Cottage Daze

Cottage Daze

James Ross

DUNDURN
A J. PATRICK BOYER BOOK
TORONTO

Project Editor: Michael Carroll
Copy Editor: Andrea Waters
Design: Courtney Horner
Printer: Webcom

Library and Archives Canada Cataloguing in Publication

Ross, James, 1960-
    Cottage daze / by James Ross.

Also issued in electronic format.
ISBN 978-1-4597-0445-9

    1. Vacation homes--Humour.
2. Country life--Humour. I. Title.

PN6231.C65R68 2012   C818'.602   C2012-900149-X

1   2   3   4   5   16   15   14   13   12

Conseil des Arts   Canada Council   ONTARIO ARTS COUNCIL
du Canada   for the Arts   CONSEIL DES ARTS DE L'ONTARIO

Canada

We acknowledge the support of the **Canada Council for the Arts** and the **Ontario Arts Council** for our publishing program. We also acknowledge the financial support of the **Government of Canada** through the **Canada Book Fund** and **Livres Canada Books**, and the **Government of Ontario** through the **Ontario Book Publishing Tax Credit** and the **Ontario Media Development Corporation**.

Care has been taken to trace the ownership of copyright material used in this book. The author and the publisher welcome any information enabling them to rectify any references or credits in subsequent editions.

J. Kirk Howard, President

Printed and bound in Canada.
www.dundurn.com

Dundurn
3 Church Street, Suite 500
Toronto, Ontario, Canada
M5E 1M2

Gazelle Book Services Limited
White Cross Mills
High Town, Lancaster, England
LA1 4XS

Dundurn
2250 Military Road
Tonawanda, NY
U.S.A. 14150

surprises. It is the opening of the cottage."
— *"Opening Day," Cottage Daze*

A collection of compassionate, humorous, and often nostalgic stories, **Cottage Daze** celebrates life in its most enjoyable sense—cottage living among family, friends, pets, and lakeside neighbours.

Who doesn't remember wading in frigid waters, helping a youngster with their first foray into waterskiing, launching a boat under the scrutiny of nearby witnesses, or getting caught in a wasp's nest? Each season brings new laughs and insights that will make readers long to get away from the bustling city to the peaceful pace of cottage country.

James Ross has a degree in journalism and has worked as a newspaper reporter, cowboy, mountain guide, museum curator, dogsledder, movie stuntman, animal trainer,

(more)

www.dundurn.com

DUNDURN

FOR IMMEDIATE RELEASE
Contact: Marta Warner
Phone: 416.214.5544 ext.222
Email: mwarner@dundurn.com

Cottage Daze

by James Ross

"Once the thick lake ice has magically transformed itself, first on a mild spring night into an infinite number of tiny ice capsules before disappearing completely the following afternoon, and once that first sunny weekend is promised in April or May … it is time. It is an

photo double, and freelance writer. He enjoys adventures and misadventures at his Muskoka island cottage in Bracebridge, Ontario.

COTTAGE DAZE
by James Ross
9781459704459
184 pages; TP
32 b&w illustrations
$19.99
PUBLICATION DATE: April 28, 2012

Also available in eBook:
ePUB: 9781459704473; $19.99
uPDF: 9781459704466; $19.99

For more information, or to speak with James Ross, please contact:
Marta Warner, Publicity Assistant, Dundurn
Phone: (416) 214-5544 ext 222

For my folks, Alan and Joyce,
for instilling in me a love and passion for cottage living.

And to my family, Chantelle, Kayla, Tori, Sean, and Jenna,
for making our island cottage such a wonderful place to write about.

Contents

Prologue: The Writer's Life

My wife will never understand the life of a writer.

Sure, she works hard. She heads off to her restaurant every day, where she slaves over the grill, settles staff issues, and deals with the demands of spoiled customers. She helps bring in the money necessary to support our family of six. I will give her that. But I work hard, too — she just doesn't always see it that way.

She comes home early from work today to find me relaxing on the back deck, sprawled out in a lounger in the sunshine. A good book lies open on my lap. A frosty beer sits on a side table, along with a pen and an empty notebook. Dark shades hide my eyes, which are shut. Many would be convinced I am sleeping, but I am simply meditating, dreaming cottage thoughts, and thinking about the summer days at the lake that will soon come.

I have filled up the kiddie pool and have it placed just off the deck beyond my bare feet. In what I thought was an inspired touch, I have taken my wife's beautiful carved wooden loon from its prestigious perch atop the fireplace mantel and have it bobbing around in the sparkling pool water.

"What are you doing?" my wife shouts, rudely awakening me from my slumbers. I try to spring to my feet, but instead, in my half-dazed state, I jump on the foot of the lounge chair. The lounger, in turn, tilts forward and springs me off the deck and into the pool with a splash. I pretend this graceful dip was my intention all along, sitting in the little wading pool splashing water over my upper torso.

If you have ever wondered what an incredulous expression looks like, all you have to do is witness the look my darling wife is giving me at this very instant. I must be a very funny sight, a big guy like me sitting in this little pool with sunglasses askew, but my spouse does not even smile. She does not even chuckle when I jump back with a little yelp, having seen a headless wooden loon swimming towards me.

"What are you doing?" she repeats, speaking very slowly and succinctly, making me for the first time realize the dangerous predicament I am now in.

"Why, I'm working," I say. Her expression of incredulity sharpens.

"Research," I try. "Writing is all about mindset." (I'm not entirely sure she is buying it.) Her hands stay fixed on her hips. I can't help but notice the colour rising, the fists clenching.

"I was suffering from a tiny bit of writer's block — and I need to have a 'Cottage Daze' column in tomorrow. I needed to get into the mood."

I sense I'm making some headway finally. I notice her head nodding slightly.

"Ah, yes, of course … then perhaps I can help," she offers graciously.

My accommodating wife quickly fetches me a gallon of deck stain and a brush. "Pretend it is the cottage porch," she says, pointing to our oversized cedar patio deck.

Later, while she has me chopping firewood, trimming trees, and raking well into the twilight hour, she bustles about in the rickety garden shed. I must admit, my wife has quite the imagination when she applies herself. With a little bit of a rustic touch, she soon has that clapboard shack looking much like an old cottage bunkhouse, complete with mice, spiders, and a thin little lumpy mattress and scratchy wool blanket for me.

"Good night," she says. "Hope this helps get you in the mood." She wanders off to our comfortable house. I light the oil lamp she has kindly provided, grab my notebook, and put pen to paper.

Yes, writing is all about mindset. Perhaps my wife understands the life of a writer, after all.

Springtime: Back to the Cottage

The Opening

It is an annual ritual that takes place once the snow has receded — not disappeared completely, but at least retreated to the protected shade of the trees. Once the thick lake ice has magically transformed itself, first on a mild spring night into an infinite number of tiny ice capsules before disappearing completely the following afternoon, and once that first sunny weekend is promised in April or May … it is time. It is an event as much anticipated by the family as Christmas morning, and is often full of as many surprises. It is the opening of the cottage.

The children are loaded into the SUV, along with the dog and enough provisions to last a year. The boat and trailer, fresh out of winter hibernation, are hooked behind. Off you go, down the highway and along the twisting, winding road to the lake. The children get carsick, the dog makes smells (or at least nobly accepts the blame), Mom snoozes, and Dad yells at the kids and chastises the pooch. Not long into the trip the first "How much farther?" and "Are we there yet?" are uttered from the back seats.

The ruckus gets louder, the dog sleeps and drools, the wife sleeps and only occasionally drools, and the dad hoarsely begs the children to quiet down. You are almost there, and the children argue over who has seen the lake first, the dog wakes up and pants out the window, the wife's eyes remain closed, and Dad's mouth lifts into a slight smile — his voice is gone. Then you arrive, in our case at the landing, which looks out at the lake and our island cottage. The dog runs in circles, the children run on the dock, and the wife wakes up and states, "That didn't take very long."

The rain starts, the wind picks up, and the water gets choppy. With everything loaded you head across the lake wondering what surprises you will find at the cabin this year.

Back at the cottage — life is good.

Thankfully, the old birch, the one that you meant to cut down in the fall, has fallen on its own but only slightly clipped the porch roof — the roof you wanted to replace this summer anyway. Worse, the ancient cedar that has stood regally for so long at the back of the privy has snapped and twisted, and is held up ever so gently in the limbs of a spindly pine, inches above the outhouse. You have to use this building, but are afraid to do so until the cedar is cleaned up, lest the branches of the pine give out while you are seated and you become always remembered on the lake as the fellow who died in this peculiar and awful fashion.

As if in celebration of your impending doom, the squirrels have decorated the building with the toilet paper you forgot to put away at closing. The mice have held a party in the cabin. Those who ice fish off your point every winter have, for whatever reason, forgotten to remove their bottles and trash. The Javex bottle left in the kitchen has frozen and exploded, and bleached the linoleum when it thawed in spring — you planned to replace the floor this summer anyway. A sack of potatoes was left in the shoe trunk over winter, which now smells only slightly more pleasant than your old runners.

The pump won't pump, the propane fridge won't light, and you forgot the liquor.

But you are back at the cottage. Life is good.

Opening Checklist

Weeks before that first trip to the cottage, I pull out the "Opening of the Cottage Checklist" from the safety of my underwear drawer in my bedroom armoire. The checklist is a yellowing, coffee-stained, crinkled piece of lined paper, with fading blue ink scrawled in my dad's handwriting. It is a list culled from years of experience, handed down from one generation to the next and updated and perfected yearly. Little notations are penned in the margins. We use it as a guideline and get ourselves more organized than we will be for any other event throughout the entire year.

My list is actually meant to remind me of what I need at the cottage. It contains items like: "Don't forget the chainsaw, sharpen it, fill the propane bottles, clean the barbecue, and bring tools, paint, brushes, and caulking for the windows. Don't forget the cabin key! Nor should you forget the starter key or the plug for the boat."

The list is also a reminder of the process I must follow after arriving. "Do a walk-around of the island and cottage, to both remind you how lucky you are and to see if anything is amiss. Turn on the propane, clean and start the fridge, assemble and prime the pump, take off the metal window screens, start barbecue, bring Muskoka chairs to dock, and then sit down and smile at wife and share a nice beverage."

My wife sees the "Opening of the Cottage Checklist" in an entirely different light. For her it is a shopping list. She takes the list as my blessing for her to go to the store to buy new things: romantic candles, tea towels, elegant yet rustic photo frames, bedding, pillows, lanterns, comforters with a bear motif, scented candles, wine glasses, candle holders, and a new opening-up-the-cabin outfit for herself. Then she looks around the garage, where we are making things ready, and decides that cardboard boxes are not really nice enough to carry these things. For this regal purpose, she knows we need those fancy plastic storage bins, those which are dreaded by husbands everywhere.

Weeks before our trip, my darling wife has everything we need stored in its place, labelled and stacked neatly ready for me to load. One plastic bin is full of linens, towels, and a couple bottles of red wine. Another contains food, and a third bin holds flashlights, candles, matches, bug spray, mousetraps, batteries, and a bottle of her favourite wine. A clear plastic bin is stacked full of toilet paper. A tall one, with newfangled locking lid latches that pop open whenever you pick it up, is crammed with every cleaning supply imaginable, and a bottle of her favourite wine.

Then there is a low, rectangular plastic bin with FIRST-AID SUPPLIES written in black marker on the top, and Band-Aids, Advil, wine, and an old Scrabble game stowed within. The Scrabble game is the same one she has been trying to beat me on for over a decade, without success. The wine is for the "without success" part.

The Advil? I believe it's for me. Most of the containers have those lids that snap shut and are purportedly childproof. When you want inside them, you are forced to use a claw hammer or pry bar to work them loose. Yet when you are transporting them across the lake in the front of your boat, the top invariably careens off and saucers through the air like a Frisbee or an ancient ninja weapon, either hitting me square on the forehead or careening higher still and clipping the tail feathers of a mallard in flight.

We won't need to eat the downed duck, however. With the lid off the bin, I'm able to see that my wife has gathered enough culinary provisions to feed an army, or to at least allow her to survive until rescued, should the lid of a container come flying off and behead me like Oddjob's bowler hat in a James Bond movie.

Start the Day

It has become known as the Cottage Breakfast. Nothing fancy, mind you, nothing gourmet. Certainly not something that you would have to suffer through, watching how to prepare it on the Food Network. Our traditional morning breakfast at the cabin is just bacon, cooked to perfection, and set gently on an English muffin, toasted golden-brown. That is it. Sometimes you can add an egg for variety. Simple, but delicious, just a traditional slice of cottage life.

It is a wonderful way to start a new day, sitting down on the dock in the early morning, watching the goings-on in the little bay out front of the cabin, while enjoying a coffee and eating this simple breakfast. Like many meals cooked at the cottage, or out on a camping trip, it tastes fantastic. Cook it at home and it just isn't the same.

My wife and I are opening up the cabin this week, and on this chilly spring morning, while I boil up some cowboy coffee and sneak in a tot of Irish cream, my wife puts the finishing touches on our first Cottage Breakfast of the year.

"It just isn't the same as when Grandpa makes it," she complains. It tastes pretty darn good to me this morning, but I know what she means. The traditional breakfast is really something that my dad started, and he is very particular about how he makes it. Grandpa does the breakfast with fastidious care. First he gets the fire going in the wood-burning cookstove, coaxing it to the proper temperature. He contends that the propane stove just won't do. Each portion is done individually. He fries up the two pieces of bacon in the cast iron frying pan and sets the English muffin halves under the broiler.

There are two minor problems associated with the Cottage Breakfast. One, cooked individually and with such attention to detail, the breakfast hour can stretch long into the late morning. His meticulous method can be a little problematic when everyone is up at the cottage at the same time, six to eight adults and seven to nine kids.

Just as Grandpa finishes feeding the early risers, the tantalizing aroma from the grill wafts into the interior of the big wall tent where the kids are sleeping, waking them in a most pleasant manner. It certainly seems to work much better than the morning alarm clock's shrill buzz that is meant to beckon them to school. One by one they will wander down to the dock and place their order. Each time that Grandpa thinks his morning task is complete, along comes another mouth to feed. Even though he complains, I think he relishes his reputation as breakfast chef extraordinaire.

The second problem? Grandpa has a certain misguided sense of chivalry. What should be first-come first-served turns into ladies first. How old-fashioned!

I try to get up early and out to the dock to be first in line. Otherwise the smoky smell of bacon frying in the skillet can drive one crazy. I have learned to bring my wife coffee in bed, hand over her book, tell her that it is still a little chilly out on the dock. "Nobody is up yet," I'll say. "Call me when you want another coffee. I'll even bring you breakfast when Grandpa gets up."

"You're not fooling anybody," she responds. "I can smell the bacon from here."

Just as the master chef is wandering down the stony path to the dock with my hot breakfast in his hand, my darling wife comes out of the boathouse bunkie, stretching and yawning.

"Oh, good morning! You're just in time, a breakfast for you," offers my charming dad. "And I'm sure your husband would love to get you a coffee," he will add.

I stomp up to the cabin. "Is that you growling, or just your stomach," teases my sensitive spouse.

It is marvellous how much we enjoy these simple pleasures in our cottage life, and interesting how things become cottage traditions. We may greet the morning with pancakes, scrambled eggs and sausages, or cereal and toast, but when that Cottage Breakfast is handed out, all of us who have spent time at our paradise experience a wonderful sense of place.

In search of those elusive trout.

Of Mice and Men

For us it's an annual battle, a constant war waged over ownership of the cottage. I'm reminded of Bill Murray's role in the movie *Caddyshack*, as a beleaguered greenskeeper trying to outwit the course-sabotaging gophers. Our nemeses are the mice that look to our cabin for shelter, comfort, and food, especially through the harsh winter months.

Keeping the cabin free from invasion is a difficult task. Whether the cottage is a posh retreat or a simple lakeside shanty, the mice do not play favourites. No matter how hard we work to "mouse-proof" the place, it is hard to stop an animal that can slip through an entrance as small as a nickel.

I was just a kid — perhaps thirteen. A mouse had been sneaking into our food cupboards, soiling the countertops, rustling the plastic bags of cereal, and waking us in the night. To catch him, I built a simple trap, a light linen cloth over a smooth-sided bucket and a cracker slathered with peanut butter for bait. Mouse, tea towel, and cracker fell into the bucket — where I found the rodent and the cloth in the morning.

"Now what?" asked my dad.

"I'll let him go outside," I said.

"He'll get back in."

"I'll take him to the other side of the island."

"He has discovered easy food. He will find his way back."

"Do I have to drown him?"

Hey, I was a sensitive kid. I paddled the one-mile stretch of water to the mainland in my canoe, a white garbage bucket in the bow. I set the mouse free. Perhaps a hawk or garter snake found him, but I felt quite pleased with myself. My dad teased me, not being able to face the facts of nature. "Outside, they are left alone," he would say. "But once our space has been invaded, they have to go."

It is with great trepidation that we head to the cabin each spring, to open the cottage for another season. What mouse treats will be left behind? What wanton acts of vandalism or destruction? What careless mistakes did we make when closing the cottage last fall?

One year a box of spaghetti had been left behind, and the mice had broken each individual noodle into tidy one-inch pieces. These they stored in various caches throughout the cabin, including inside the oven mitts that hung on the side of the stove. Another year it was a bar of soap, left by the sink, that was chewed and shaved into a thousand slivers, leaving us with the freshest smelling rodents on the lake.

This year, Grandma is annoyed that someone has stolen the laces out of her old, comfortable camp shoes — though nobody will admit to needing a piece of string. We find the thieves when we separate the box spring and mattress in the back bedroom. The laces are there, still in one piece, wound gently around the lip of a downy mouse nest, like garland around a Christmas wreath. Mouse mom and mouse babies stare up in innocence. The children find them cute — our youngest asks to keep one, wanting to name him Stuart Little. The war is at a truce.

With the grandchildren and Grandma keeping a stern watch, and I, for my part, grinning a silly smile that hinges on a thirty-some-year-old cottage memory, off goes Grandpa in the boat to shore, with a family of mice gently stowed with their nest in a bucket at the bow.

Hello, World!

My dad would wander out on the front porch of the cottage and shout out, "Hello, world!" at the top of his lungs. The bellow would break the silence of a summer's evening and echo across the still lake waters. I am not sure if anyone across on shore ever heard him, but they certainly didn't bother to holler back with, "Hello, Mr. Ross." Maybe they just heard it and muttered amongst themselves, "There's that lunatic again."

We would have just finished up our dinner when he'd get up and step outside to let go with his familiar salutation. Or we might be playing a family board game on the big pine harvest table in the evening when he would head out to the loo, pausing on the porch to shout.

Sometimes we kids would have settled in for the night in the boathouse bunkie. We would be telling ghost stories or shining our flashlights around on the ceiling like spotlights. We would be giggling and talking and, sometimes, we would be getting yelled at to "be quiet and get to sleep and quit wasting the batteries in the flashlights!" — much the same things we chastise our kids for now. When we had settled down and were drifting off to a sweet sleep, lulled by the sounds of waves lapping on shore, the wind in the trees, or the distant call of a loon, comforted even by the sounds of adult voices and laughter coming from the cottage — suddenly the front door of the cabin would swing open and we would hear the familiar refrain, "Hello, world!"

When we were young we would giggle at his antics. What a silly thing for a dad to be doing. In our teenage years we would roll our eyes and think, "How geeky!" As we grew older and visited the cottage with our friends, we would wince every time he stepped outside, and then let out a sigh of relief if nothing happened. Then, there it was, the shout. He seemed curiously incapable of being embarrassed, which was all right because I felt enough for both of us. Red-faced, I would cast an eye at my comrades for their reactions.

In retrospect, though I might have thought his antics embarrassed me in front of my good friends, I don't think his inane shouting from the cottage's front porch elicited any such response from them. Perhaps their own fathers had similar unusual traits. Perhaps they had become hardened to such behaviour over time.

When I started visiting the cottage with my own family, Grandpa would still wander out to the front porch and shout his greeting. The kids would giggle; what a funny thing for a grandpa to be doing. I was all right with it by then, too. In fact, his shouted greeting had become a part of the place, a part of what I felt at home and comfortable with and what made the cottage such a familiar and fun place to visit.

We bought the cottage from my folks, and a funny thing happened. I would step outside in the evening, and I'd have this overpowering desire to shout to the world. At first I'd send out the familiar phrase in a hoarse

Feel as if you can fly.

whisper. Sometimes I'd yell it a little louder, much to my children's chagrin and my wife's displeasure. She'd give me that look: "See, you're turning into your dad, you're picking up all his silly habits. Do you want me to start acting like my mom?" Well, no, but that's another whole column.

We opened up the cottage on a beautiful weekend in April this year. We had made our way through the opening checklist, completed our chores, and then sat down for a nice steak dinner. We cleaned up afterwards, together, and then I stepped out on the porch, stretched, and couldn't resist the urge … "Hello, world!" I shouted.

My wife stepped out behind me, but rather than giving me heck, she gave me a little hug and said, "Yes, it's great to be back here."

Looking back, I realize that my dad's greeting, offered out to the lake, was simply a statement to anyone who was listening and to nobody in particular. My dad was saying, "I'm happy to be here!" Or perhaps, "I love this place!" After all, he never did it anywhere else. It was something only for the cottage. "Hello, world!"

The Rescue

First of all, before I begin this little story, I want to let it be known that I do not suffer from arachnophobia. I might prefer a snake slithering across my path, a leech stuck to my midsection, or even tripping over a hornets' nest to having a big, hairy, creepy-crawling spider spinning me into a death cocoon, but, in general, spiders are all right.

The Hobbses are good friends of ours. Even though they live over a mile away, they are our cottage neighbours. They have the small island called Blueberry to the northeast. If we ever need a hand, or advice, Harvey Hobbs is always willing.

This April the lake ice took away the dock on Blueberry Island, making it extremely difficult for the Hobbses to land on their steep rock shoreline. The dock had simply disappeared, another victim of the destructive power of spring breakup. Here, then, was an opportunity for us to pay back the Hobbses for their unerring helpfulness. We set out on a morning mission in our boat to find the missing dock and return it to its rightful place. After some searching, we spied an intact, sixteen-foot section of the dock on an uninhabited stretch of the north shore.

The dock was wedged high on the boulder-strewn beach. My wife and I struggled to get it afloat, using twelve-foot rails as pry bars. My father, skippering the boat, attached a line to the stringers and pulled. We gradually worked the heavy thing loose and got it floating. My wife jumped into the bow of the runabout to help guide us through the many shoals. I stayed on the dock-turned-raft.

Off we went, towing the dock across the calm lake with me balancing on the deck boards. If I moved towards the bow, the front of the dock dipped below the water. If I moved to the port or starboard, I found I could help manoeuvre the clumsy barge to the left or right. Only the back middle third of the dock stayed high and dry.

Imagine my consternation when, as I stood regally on the raft with the wind blowing through my hair, I looked down and saw an enormous spider standing beside me. He looked like my pet dog sitting primly there at my feet. If I was captain of this vessel, he was my first mate. He was huge and ugly. I wouldn't say he was as big as my hand (that would be an exaggeration) but he wasn't much smaller. I was naturally startled, which is why I let out a little screech, a piercing whelp that thankfully went unheard over the buzz of the boat motor. I quickly regained my composure and almost decided to squish him, sending his body to a watery grave.

I admired his bravery, however. I admired his survival instincts. He had joined me on this little adventure, so who was I to repay his trust by stamping down on him with my water shoes. Besides, I felt like Pi on a raft alone with his Bengal tiger. Oh, you may laugh, me comparing this little insect to a ferocious killer cat, but spiders can be extremely dangerous, too.

So the journey continued for this spider and me, two castaways separated from certain death by a few dry boards. I kept a watchful eye on him — and sensed that he did the same with me. When I looked nervously down, he craned his little head and peered skyward. I smiled, and he returned the grin. The trip seemed to last for most of the day, but in reality took about an hour. Finally we circled around Blueberry Island and motored into the little nook to return the dock to its old resting spot.

The boat crew released the tow rope and threw me a paddle so I could steer our dock into position. As I leaned over to paddle, the dock dipped under the lake water. The spider headed for high ground, which just happened to be up my leg. I swatted him.

Now, before you get upset at my reaction, thinking that I had killed my faithful travelling companion, when I say "swatted him" I simply mean I brushed him off my leg. True, my action did send him catapulting into the lake, causing him to thrash about in a dance of survival, but it was a predicament that was easily rectified with a gently placed paddle blade. The arachnid climbed aboard, and I placed him gently on shore. Without a word of thanks, he scurried off.

I hope that Harvey is happy to have his dock back, and that he does not mind that I have added to the spider population of his island. I'm sure he will happily bound off his dock, up onto the island, and walk face first into a sticky spiderweb. Perhaps it was a pregnant female.

Flying Piranha

My wife is from Vancouver. There are no blackflies in Vancouver — none in the whole of British Columbia, really. There are plenty of mosquitoes. There are little gnats we call no-see-ums that get under the brim of your hat and bite at your forehead. There are wasps and hornets and bees, and ticks that drop off the spring willow and burrow into your neck. Big horseflies dart around your head, avoiding your windmilling arms, driving you slowly crazy.

There are biting red ants that crawl up your socks and nip at your ankles when you unwittingly sit on a rotten log or lie out in the grass on a warm summer's day using their anthill as a pillow. There are many minor nuisances in our western province, but none that can measure up to the ferocity of the blackfly. Blackflies prefer the rocks, lakes, bush, and swift-flowing streams of Muskoka. They are a little bit like cottagers that way.

While I have fond memories of these miniature flying piranha from my youth, when we move back to cottage country in the summer of 2005, my wife has yet to be introduced.

"There is something wrong with Jenna," cries my wife. "She's bleeding from the back of her head." She holds our six-year-old daughter close to comfort her, but her panic and the mention of blood serves only to agitate the youngster, sending her into tears.

I wander over to have a look. Little trickles of blood stream down from behind each ear.

"Did you hit your head?" my wife is asking.

"Blackflies," I pronounce. Of course, I am always quite pleased to know something about something. Especially to know some little tidbit that my wife does not. It happens so rarely.

"Blackflies did that?" she asks incredulously — and then she takes a swat at a deer fly that has landed on our daughter's back. "Well, there is one blackfly that won't be bothering you again," she states haughtily, as the crumpled fly falls dead to the grass.

"No, no," say I — and I point to a tiny little flying speck that buzzes Jenna's hair.

My wife squints at the minuscule gnat and then stares at me as if I am quite mad. The little black insects cloud around my head as well, landing on the hairline at the back of my neck. I stupidly let one take a huge chunk out of my hide, just to prove my point. She watches the blood flow, and then starts to laugh. Cheered by the sudden gaiety, my young daughter also giggles at my misfortune, and the two ladies trot happily into the cottage to clean up the bloody smears, leaving me to wave my hands frantically at a swarming, invisible enemy.

While blackflies love me, they do not seem to care for my wife. When we work around the cabin, she does so in shorts and T-shirt, while I cover up, flail my arms about inanely, and constantly twitch and shake like a dog. Why blackflies prefer some people to others, I do not know. Perhaps it is because, though she is of the fair sex, I have the fairer skin. I have told her that her blood must be sour — to which she retorts that most flying insects do seem to swarm over horse droppings in the field.

The Game of Tape and Ladders

Okay, here's the deal: I'm swinging on the cabin's main log beam, looking a lot like Cheetah, the chimpanzee. Perhaps I am dating myself here.

Cheetah was Tarzan's pet monkey in those 1930s black and white Tarzan movies, the chimp who was so talented at swinging on branches and from tree to tree. Maybe my audience for this column is a little younger; I should have compared myself to Rafiki, the famous blue-faced baboon of *Lion King* fame — or perhaps George of the Jungle.

Anyway, I'm wasting time here, and time is something I don't feel I have a lot of in my current predicament — so back to my story …

I'm swinging on the big log purloin that runs the length of our cottage. I was cleaning the large upper front window when the ladder underneath me essentially collapsed.

Swinging around, holding on for dear life, and looking down at the floor far beneath, I sense that my wife is standing there laughing at me. She seems to be asking, "What do you think you are doing?" Then, perhaps showing a tiny bit of compassion, she seems to be asking if I'm all right. It's like it is not unusual for her to hear a crash, come into the cabin, and see her husband swinging on the ceiling like a primate.

It seems like hours, but is more likely just a few seconds that I hang there speechless — speechless until I realize she is trying to coax me down with a banana. "Please hurry out to the shed and grab the old wooden ladder," I plead.

"That old thing?" she asks. "That's dangerous."

"Dear, my arm is getting tired here."

She rescues me with the aged, warped wooden ladder, the one with the split rail and missing rungs, the ladder that she has been asking me to throw out or burn for years. Instead, I kept it as a backup (and I'm sure glad I did) for the more modern aluminum stepladder, the one that was held together with duct tape, the one that my father-in-law had rescued from the dump and bequeathed to me at the time of my marriage. Perhaps he hoped we would elope. Or perhaps he hoped the ladder would collapse into a mangle of metal with me on it, as it did just now.

Safe on the ground, and feeling lucky, I expect a few tears and a hug of gratitude from my darling spouse, who came so close to losing me. Instead, I find myself being chastised. "We're getting a new ladder. I've been telling you to throw those ladders out for years!" This anger comes from being truly afraid, I try telling myself, until, "It could have been me on that ladder, did you ever think of that?"

It is funny. Our cottage often becomes the retirement home for all of our old tools and furniture, stuff that has long worn out its welcome at home. When my wife says, "We have to get rid of that before someone gets hurt," I slip it into my pickup and sneak it up to the cottage. I might find the available funds to buy some nice steaks and a good bottle of wine for the cottage barbecue dinner, I might even splurge on that bottle of rare single malt to enjoy on the dock at day's end, but a few bucks for a new ladder? I've got one that works — I even have a backup.

As she continues chastising, my wife notices that my concentration is waning. Worse than that, she always seems to know what I'm thinking. My gaze has shifted to the scrap of metal that was once a sturdy ladder — thirty-some years earlier, perhaps. I'm thinking, "With a few wooden splints and a lot of duct tape, we just might get a few more years out of" ... *whap*. I survived the fall, only to be concussed by a ripe banana.

Forever Young

It is astonishing the sharp, distinct, and compelling memories that summer cottages evoke.

I had been living out west for more than twenty years when my parents decided it was time to sell our family island cottage. I knew, then, it was time to come home. We were a family of wanderers, never living in one town too long, always off in search of a new adventure. As we moved from place to place, the cottage remained a constant and was where I felt most rooted. I didn't want to lose it. So I bought the property, loaded up my life, and drove across the country.

Now, when I see my own children climbing up swim rock in their bathing suits, I experience a strong sense of déjà vu. I watch them and remember my young cottage days, when our pleasant summer routine had us spending our days swimming, playing board games, loafing, running in the trees, water-skiing, building bonfires, and, as we got older, flirting with young ladies.

When the low black rain clouds rolled in across the lake and the thunder and lightning whipped the water into a frenzy, we lit the oil lamps and spent our afternoons and evenings in the cabin or out on the covered porch, reading, conversing, or playing games. There was a certain simplicity to our life there: we pulled out old board games, a deck of cards, or warped jigsaw puzzles.

We ran through the island's dark spruce and balsam forest, feeling that we had discovered a place of mystery and wonder. In this quiet wood we sensed the primeval and thought that no one had stood here before. We found our own hideouts and secret bases, hollows under thick boughs, mini caves hidden under granite ledges.

The cottage is a place of youth and energy.

As the summer progressed, our tans darkened and our messy, tangled hair was streaked blond from the sun. We were like shipwrecked children with our own customs and rituals. Our parents were mere ghosts. We had no watches, and there was no clock on the cabin wall. When we were hungry, we gathered on swim rock for lunch and then returned to the water or the dark forest.

I remember our driftwood fires on the point, where we sang and laughed, told ghost stories, and exchanged intimacies — so now, whenever I see bonfire embers glowing, I am brought back to those days. At the end of the night, when silence had fallen over us, we trudged back to the cabin, feeling our way past the roots and rocks of the dirt trail.

Now I watch my children with their siblings, cousins, and friends, running through the same forest that I ran through as a child. They find the same hideouts and forts. Their imaginations lead them into similar games. They become pirates, knights on a quest, warlords, or frontiersmen. They paddle to nearby Sawdust Island, claiming it as their own, guarding it against all trespassers. They pack a picnic lunch, and we give them a cowbell to clang in case of trouble.

These little things are touchstones for cottage memories and proof that a summer home is not a place like anywhere else. It is a place of youth and energy — where we spent many happy, wonderful summers. The cottage that we visit now is not necessarily the geographical one of the present, but the one of my youth, and everywhere I look, the ghost of my old self is present.

The Breakdown and the Brat

Why is it that your boat never breaks down tied up to your own dock, but always waits until you are in the middle of the lake?

My sister's family had arrived and I ran down to the dock, jumped in the boat, and started the engine. I spun the boat around with a flourish, and then roared across the one-kilometre stretch of water towards the shore to ferry them and their gear across to the cottage. Halfway there, the motor made a loud clunk and stopped. This did not sound good.

Handyman that I am, I checked the battery connections, though I knew that this problem was worse than that. I lifted the motor and inspected the prop. I took off the cover and made a theatrical display of checking over the motor, even though I did not have a clue what I was doing. The boat drifted in the wind, destined for the far east arm of the lake. I pulled out the paddle and tried to set a course back to our island.

I imagined my sister and her husband on shore, hands on their hips, saying, "Now, what's he doing?"

I dipped the paddle and pulled hard, trying to fight against wind and wave. Why are they never with you when you are in such a predicament? I did not hope for rescue by some observant cottager on the mainland; I only wished not to be seen. I saw my wife paddling in my direction with the kayak.

"What are you doing?" said she.

"Oh, just paddling my motorboat."

She hooked a tow rope from kayak to runabout, and then she paddled hard towards our cottage. I yelled directions to her. "Harder! More to the left. No, right. Put your back into it!"

Then I saw a boat approaching. Feeling bad to be caught with my wife working so hard, I untied her tow rope and set her free; she took several easy strokes away and then turned in surprise.

"Nothing you can do here, honey," I shouted loudly. "You go on back to your lounger on the dock and I'll be there momentarily. Whoa, what's this? Oh, a boat to the rescue." I saw that the rental boat was being driven by my brother-in-law, and realized that my dramatic presentation had been wasted. He was smiling — hero to the rescue. He pulled me to shore and headed back for his crew.

After we had gone over the motor and realized that there was nothing that we, in our wisdom, were capable of fixing, I ran the rental craft back to the resort to make arrangements to keep it for a few days. The owner had just pulled up in his ATV with a trailer full of kindling. His six-year-old grandson was loading a few sticks of the wood onto a remote control Hummer and steering it into their cabin to the woodbox. Sometimes the miniature vehicle lost control navigating over the door jamb and spilled its load on the welcome mat. The boy pretended to be the road crew, reloading the scattered wood.

Why does your boat always wait until you're in the middle of the lake to break down?

"That's a neat way to do that," I said.

"Hi, dummy," said the boy.

"Pardon?"

"Wasn't it you stuck out on the lake?"

Before I could answer, the grandpa was there, reprimanding the youngster for his cheek with a client. I envisioned him standing with the boy earlier and saying, "Look at that dummy stuck with his boat out in the middle of the lake." I settled up for the boat and headed back to the dock in a huff. Flustered, I pulled and pulled on the cord, and flooded the little outboard.

"You don't even know how to drive a boat!" the precocious six-year-old shouted.

"Shush," said his grandpa.

What's Eating You?

Standing on the sidelines of the local soccer field last night watching my daughter's game, I came to the realization that, here in cottage country, we enjoy a real home field advantage. We are used to the cloud of blackflies and mosquitoes that harass us; the other team is not. Our girls stand firm, used to the fog of pesky insects and prepared beforehand with a slathering of bug spray. The other team is driven to distraction. My problem is I don't like covering myself in chemicals, but I don't relish being eaten alive either.

A family friend frequently visits us in Muskoka from the Falkland Islands. I am sure not many Falklanders visit cottage country on a frequent basis, but he is partial to our beautiful landscape. In the Falklands there are no bugs: no blackflies, mosquitoes, wasps, or hornets. I think it has something to do with the South Atlantic winds, which blow constant and fierce, sending any pesky flying intruders catapulting westward to the South American continent.

Danny does not like snow and cold, so I invite him here in June with the promise of sparkling clear lakes, the smell of wildflowers, and warm, sunny days. I do not mention that the sweet gifts of nature in spring have a decidedly nasty side. First comes the cloud of blackflies, buzzing around our heads and nibbling behind our ears, arriving in mid-May and hanging out until the children are released from school in late June. As the blackfly attacks wane, the mosquitoes are out in full force, having arrived in the rains of late May, overstaying their welcome into July.

It is the time of year when these biting insects try to chase us indoors, reminding us that we may not actually be at the pinnacle of the food chain, but rather at the top of the menu. They buzz our decks and gardens, pester us at the barbecue, and ruin our golf games (or at least are blamed). They find us at the lake, accompany us over the portage, and act as companions on our hikes. For as long as people have sought adventure beyond the city, the blackflies and mosquitoes have tested our ingenuity.

I ask every conceivable type of outdoor worker how they attempt to combat these nuisances of nature: a ranger in Algonquin Park, a forester, a hydro lineman, and a fishing guide. I approach the elderly lady in the cottage down the road who seems to spend all of her waking hours with her gnomes in the flower garden. I even query Health Canada. They all give variations of the same answer: "Wear long pants tucked into socks and a light-coloured, long-sleeved shirt with a collar, and, if you do not mind looking like a dork, a head net and peaked cap offers effective protection. Oh, and slather on the DEET."

My Falkland Islander and I are determined to find a natural, green alternative to take back the outdoors. Well, actually, Danny has no clue, but it is my mission with him as bait. I will send my friend out into the breach, knowing that the mosquitoes and blackflies will gather from miles around, attracted, like Dracula, to this virgin blood source. Some might think me cruel; I call it research.

Biting insects are attracted to dark clothing. I buy Danny a black sweatshirt and don a white tee myself, before asking him to help me pile some firewood. I am left in relative peace, while Danny twitches, flails his arms, and swats his hands at an invisible enemy. Finally, with a cry, he runs off in search of some repellent. In his absence, the blackflies turn their attentions to me, making me realize that, though they may be attracted to dark clothing, if the only food available is the Man from Glad, they are not fussy eaters.

Perfumes, soaps, scented products, and hairsprays entice the biting flies. Danny has no hair, so hairspray is out, but I do convince him that Axe body scent not only attracts the ladies as much as they show in the commercials, it also repulses the flying pests. He soaks himself in it, ventures outside, and is swarmed by a cloud of females.

If you are thinking that I put all the research onus on my assistant, let me say that I also do my part. Since the biting bugs are attracted to the ammonia in sweat, I try lazing around instead of working, and, because mosquitoes are attracted to carbon dioxide, I suggest to my wife that she should try talking as little as possible while outdoors. Neither tactic is entirely successful.

Garlic apparently wards off more than vampires. It acts on the insect's sensory capabilities, overwhelming them so they can't smell the carbon dioxide and lactic acid that attracts them to humans. A concentrated garlic spray applied on plants, trees, and lawns may have your homestead smelling like an Italian restaurant, but it is somewhat successful. Try eating fresh garlic or a capsule of garlic powder every day. Unfortunately, this also overwhelms my wife's sensory capabilities.

With the love of spring lost I turn to brewer's yeast, feeling that this is finally something I can work with. In fact, I spend more time researching this bug deterrent than any other suggested to me. I'm not sure it succeeds. After ingesting a few bottles, I believe the bugs are just as interested in me, but I don't really care.

Technology has taken over most facets of our lives, so it is not a surprise that it has involved itself in the battle of the bugs. CO_2-based machines seem to work, provided they are positioned properly. We hook one up by the house, and I serve Danny his afternoon tea on the deck. In minutes he is being eaten alive, and I realize that the mosquitoes, attracted to the machine, pass by a pre-dinner appetizer. Remember to place the machine between the area to be protected and the area the mosquitoes are coming from.

While most of us do not appreciate biting flies, we must always remember they are an important part of the ecosystem. Birds, bats, and fish feed on them. Blackfly larvae are a sign of unpolluted waters, and it has been thought that the adults pollinate our beloved blueberries. And they have been called the region's best conservationists — protecting wilderness from larger numbers of human trespassers.

My former friend Danny? The mosquitoes and blackflies might keep the less hardy away, but in his estimation the beauty of cottage country is worth some minor irritation. The only things that do really work for him are a netted suit that has him looking like a beekeeper, his self-roll cigarettes that keep everything away, and a heavy supply of AfterBite to deal with the inevitable attacks. Oh, and a late-afternoon Muskoka breeze that has him dreaming about the Falkland wind.

Nature's Guardians

I attended the Spring Cottage Life Show in April. Yes, it is a show for dreaming — about that ultimate ski boat or sporty little sailboat, a new gazebo or sauna, a mobile drinks bar that follows you around, or that space-age, composting toilet. Okay, I don't really dream about the toilet. There are toys and there are more toys, all meant to make your cottage experience more luxurious, more enjoyable, more exciting, and infinitely more comfortable.

When I had mentally used up my next year's salary on gimmicks and playthings, it was the new green trend that caught my attention. Well, it's not that new, but it does seem to be finally taking a firm foothold in our cottage behaviour. I know for too many years, for many of us the word "green" conjured up negative images of a utilitarian, uncomfortable retreat. I think we have finally began to realize that if we do not take steps to help preserve the natural beauty that surrounds us at our cottages, it might be lost to our children and future generations. As cottagers, we are privileged to share in the natural environment, but at the same time, we have a responsibility as nature's guardians.

Far too often in the past, people have bought cottages for their wilderness value, and then tried to tame that wilderness. The process seemed logical. We would just tidy the place up a bit, make it more visually appealing and less of a mosquito haven. We would cut out the long grass and reeds that framed the beach along the shoreline. We would bring in some fine sand to make the beach seem more tropical.

We would thin the trees, cut back the bramble and undergrowth, plant some grass seed or bring in some sod to replace what we had removed, build a concrete retaining wall to separate lawn from sand, and then put down some chemicals to prevent the weeds from regaining a foothold. The cottage now looks tidy and cared for. Our view to the water has been enhanced, and the number of flying insects has been reduced.

We get so busy admiring and tending our manicured grounds and comfortable waterfront that we do not immediately notice that the ducks, mergansers, herons, and loons do not come around as much as they used to. The songbirds, who had brightened our mornings with their music, do not seem to be quite as exuberant. The frogs, too, no longer keep up their end in that beautiful symphony of the night. We blame these problems on global warming, lack of government environmental initiatives, or the wake from those unruly motorboats that zip past. Seldom do we look at ourselves as part of the problem.

But what can we do?

The truth of the matter is that the greenest thing you can do for nature is often just to leave it alone. In a cottage environment, that is, of course, impossible — but it is imperative that we minimize the disruption. Through urbanization we have banished, either deliberately or inadvertently, the abundant plant and animal life that lived there before our arrival. We must not let this happen at the cottage. While native plant life absorbs most surface water, over half the rainwater that falls on your manicured cottage lawn pours right over the grass and into the water, carrying with it any harmful fertilizers and pesticides.

To me, leaving things as they are sounds like the ultimate lazy man's plan. I can chuck my "honey-do" list and head to the Muskoka chair on the dock, accompanied by my brand new, handy-dandy, mobile, follow-you-around bar.

Farewell to a Cottage Friend

I lost a good friend on the May long weekend. I wouldn't say it was sudden; old age had set in, so it was not totally unexpected. Still, it came as a shock, and it certainly put a damper on our first visit to the cottage this year.

Worse, it was partially my fault. I ask myself, would he have stayed around a little longer if I had not been so rough with him? Perhaps I could have shown more tender, loving care. A thorough cleaning once in a while might have helped. He worked hard, he was efficient, and when done, what would I do in return? I would take what he offered and then shut him up, leave him standing there alone while I escaped to the comfort of the cabin to sit around with family and friends, talking, laughing, and dining. When a storm blew in, I would run off to the shelter of the cottage without a thought for him drenched in the rain. Often, I didn't even bother to cover him up.

I am getting a tear in my eye now, just thinking about him. He was strong, unpretentious, loyal, and reliable. He was really nothing to look at. He was a bit greasy and sometimes smelled a little gassy. He moved about with a little bit of a limp in his later years. He had certain quirks and mannerisms that you just learned to accept, deal with, and work around. He was unbalanced, and his knob didn't work properly. But he never let me down.

He was twenty-six years old when he finally bit it. Now, that doesn't sound very old in human terms, but for a barbecue it is ancient. I know how old he was because we kids had given him to my parents on their twenty-fifth wedding anniversary. They celebrated their fiftieth last May. He spent some time at our family home, and then he was shuffled off to the cottage when a fancy brand name barbecue came along.

I do not remember feeling too bad for him, because the cottage is a nice place to retire. He didn't want to retire, though, so he soldiered on. We would throw him in the dark, dank shed for winter, and then we'd pull him out upon our return to the cottage in spring. He never seemed to mind; actually, he seemed thrilled to see us. I'd throw on a propane tank and stand out there with him, flipping steaks or sausages or burgers. I would drink a cold beer and feed him a little bit of sauce. When he was done, I would give him a little scratch on the head with a wire brush, and he was content.

I hope you don't mind me, in these politically correct times, calling this trusted outdoor cooking implement a he, but a barbecue just seems to me to be a masculine thing. He was always there when I needed him. He was great for my self-esteem. I have always been a little inept around the kitchen, but when I was partnered with him I could cook up whatever my wife sent my way. She could hand me a platter of chicken, beef, or ribs — no problem.

At home, three or four barbecues came and went. These shiny new appliances helped out for a little time, and then meekly packed it in. Even with all their bells and whistles and hefty price tags, they had nothing on our old comrade. When I bought the family cottage, I insisted that the purchase include this faithful friend. Perhaps it was cottage life that prolonged his existence; the beauty, the fresh air, the peacefulness. It seemed like he would live forever.

This spring, my wife set out a plate of T-bones, so off I went to the storage shed. I yanked him out … and then it happened. His top fell off, his body disintegrated into dust. I stood there, stunned and sad. Holding my hand was a wooden handle; it was all that was left of my friend.

I wandered into the cottage looking woeful and forlorn, and my wife could tell instantly something had happened.

"What's wrong?" she asked.

"He's gone," I croaked. "Can you throw those steaks on the broiler?"

Boat Launch

It was a bit of a Mr. Bean moment. I had unstrapped the boat from the trailer and then backed it down into the water at the public boat launch. I jumped out of the car, went around back, released the winch, and unhooked the winch rope from the ring on the boat's bow. It was then that I realized that I had not backed up quite far enough to get the boat afloat and free from the trailer. So I jumped back into the vehicle and inched it another foot backwards into the lake. The boat drifted free and floated out into the bay.

I stood there with my hands on my hips looking at my boat floating fifteen feet off shore. I tried to coax it in. "Come here, little boat," I muttered. I thought about paddling my hands in the water, drawing them inwards to create a current that would pull the boat in, but decided that, although this technique works in the bathtub with my toy battleships or yellow ducky, it was not likely to work here in this big lake with a sixteen-foot runabout.

I used to be pretty good with a lariat in my horseman days, but the only rope I had of any length was stowed neatly in the boat's storage locker. What to do? The breeze seemed to be picking up, ruffling the water and pushing the boat away. I didn't even have my swim shorts with me. I looked around: nobody was there, no one was around to bear witness to my foolhardiness. In that respect, at least, it was my lucky day. I removed my shoes, rolled up my jeans, and stepped gingerly into the lake.

I thought if I were able to walk out to my knees and then stretch my arms fully, I might just be able to reach. I sloshed out deeper, but the boat seemed to be drifting away at the same speed. I was past my knees, then the cold water was cooling my tender regions, causing me to walk on tiptoes. Soon I was swimming, doing the breast stroke until I reached a dragging boat line. I turned and towed the boat towards shore.

I remembered the time when I had been so excited, and in such a rush to get over to our island cottage, that I had arrived at the launch and backed the boat in, forgetting to put the plug in the vessel. I backed it down into the water, unhooked it, got it started, and ran it over to the dock to load our gear and provisions. An old-timer standing there with a fishing line in the water, barely giving me any notice, mumbled almost incoherently, "Yer boat seems to be ridin' low, young fella." A pause to spit some tobacco. "Appears to be sinking — sure you 'membered the plug?"

As I swam, fully clothed, for shore, I consoled myself with the fact that at least this time, my act of stupidity had gone unseen. Too soon, as it turned out. I was halfway back, stretching my toes to feel the bottom, when I heard an approaching truck. I panicked and swam hard. Unfortunately, tugging a boat along slows you down. I was still a ways out when the vehicle came into view. I froze and dropped low in the water: "Please don't look this way."

A sister's boat is asking to be hijacked.

My heart sank. It was the Brat and his grandpa, the same grandpa we had rented a boat from when our boat had broken down in the middle of the lake. It was the same precocious youngster who had called me a dummy, who had said that I didn't know what I was doing when it came to boats.

The truck stopped and their heads slowly, and in unison, turned my way. Realizing that hiding was futile, I gave them a little wave, like I take my boat for a swim everyday.

"Grandpa, what's that dummy doing now?" I heard the Brat's voice through the truck's open window.

"Hush," said Grandpa. And then he yelled out the window to me, "Need a hand?"

"No. No, I'm good. Just checking for leaks," I tried, knowing all too well that by evening, at the latest, my folly would be common knowledge around the lake.

"Grandpa?"

"Hush," he said again, and they drove on.

The Robin

Once upon a midday dreary, while I pondered, weak and weary, over many a quaint and curious volume of forgotten lore. While I nodded, nearly napping, suddenly there came a tapping, as of someone gently rapping, rapping at my cottage door.

I heard the tapping, but could not immediately place the noise. It sounded like one of the kids playing a joke, tapping on the cabin door and interrupting my work. I yelled for quiet, but then realized I was being dim-witted: I was at the cottage myself this time. Still, my bellow had the desired effect and the outside world was once again peaceful.

I peered out the big dining room window at the front porch of the cabin, but seeing nothing I returned to my work. Before too long, the noise started up again, *tap, tap, tap.*

I got up from the table and looked out the window … nothing. With a furrowed brow I threw open the door. On the porch stood a robin — just a robin and nothing more. I jumped back with a start. Not that I am afraid of a robin, of course, but having such a bird knocking at my cottage door was slightly eerie. The robin, seeing me, also gave a start, dropped a thread of dead grass from her beak, and flew off with a squawk.

I looked around, smiled, then shut the door. I returned to my laptop and began tapping away myself. With no repeat of the rapping on the door, I soon got back into the rhythm of my work. During a brief pause and deep in thought, I gazed out over the beautiful lake. Suddenly I was greeted by the horrifying spectacle of a dark shape hurtling itself against the large window. I jumped up and ran to look, expecting to see a poor, stunned bird lying dying on the cottage porch.

Instead, I saw my robin. She hopped up on the armrest of the hewn log rocking chair, peered briefly in at me, and then suddenly assaulted the windowpane once again. I stared wide-eyed. Again and again she repeated the manoeuvre, hurtling herself at the window, falling back on the wood porch, and hopping back on the chair, before doing it all again.

The robin was stark raving mad, I was convinced of that. She was half cuckoo bird.

I had a sudden, horrible vision of her breaking the glass window and then attacking me where I stood, pecking me to death. I opened the door and shooed her away. She flew to a nearby tree and from there screeched at me, as if I were the crazy one.

I returned to my table but could no longer focus on any work. Time and time again, the robin returned to the porch, repeating her ridiculous attacks on the window. I tried shutting the curtains, to no avail. I tried moving the chair away, but this only served to eliminate one stage of her attack. I found a roll of masking tape and stuck strips across the glass panes, but this only slowed her for a while.

I looked around for ideas. I contemplated taping a photo of my wife to the window, but knew instinctively that even if this worked I would lose. I took the book jacket off a Rick Mercer Report book I was reading and taped the photo of Rick onto the glass. All was quiet. I looked out: the robin had retreated into the trees.

I felt quite alone the rest of the day and evening, and suffered through a restless night. I was up early the next morning, and when I opened the door a crack to look out I scared the robin away from her window perch. She had built a neat nest on the ledge, under the cover photo of Rick Mercer, his forehead only slightly whitewashed.

I had come up to the cottage by myself this time to do some cottage chores and to get some peaceful work time in, before the kids were out of school for summer holidays. I realize now why I have always insisted the cottage is meant to be a family place — it is a scary place to visit alone.

The Nesting Box

A neighbouring cottager gave me a nesting box a few years back. It was of simple wood construction, two feet high, one foot wide, and one foot deep, with an entry hole cut out in the upper front and a slanted roof that could be removed for cleaning. Following his instructions, I filled the box with clean straw in the autumn and nailed it onto a leaning birch tree, about ten feet from the ground and six feet back from the lakeshore. I'm not sure I expected anything.

The following spring, upon our return to the cottage and after all our opening chores were done, I spied the lonely box high in the tree and decided it was vacant. I wondered about hanging an "Apartment for Rent" sign. I climbed the rickety cottage ladder to see if anything, any animal or bird, had taken the time to check out the premises. I peered in the round entry door and was immediately taken aback by two glowing eyes and a terrifying hiss from within, a demonic sound that had me falling backwards from my stoop into the shallow lake waters.

For three springs running, the box was occupied. Each fall I would clean it and fill it with fresh straw, and each spring the female would be nesting. It is wonderful having a family of mergansers darting this way and that in our quiet bay, hiding out under the boathouse or in the grass and shrubs along the shoreline, a string of little chicks trailing after an attentive mother. This summer, our mergansers are absent.

My dog smelled the problem first. I saw her sitting at the foot of the birch, staring up at the wooden box, tilting her head this way and that and sniffing the air. At first I thought there must be a mother with chicks, and ordered the dog away. Then I smelled the sulfury stench of bad eggs. I carefully climbed the ladder and peered in. Sadly, I found nine eggs in the nest, abandoned and rotting. Either the mother had simply left her eggs or, more likely, she had met an unfortunate end: a fox, wolf, angry loon, or crazed boater. As landlord and owner of the nesting box, I felt partially responsible for the loss.

We try to help out Mother Nature in little ways. Feeders are hung from tree branches, their seed kept replenished for the songbirds that sing the praises of each new day. Hummingbird stations are kept filled with sweet nectar and hung off the porch. Bat houses are built to attract the night flyers, who in turn keep the mosquito population in check. Nesting

Build it, and they will come.

boxes are strategically placed on trees along the rocky shoreline. All are kept clean, fresh, sanitized, and in good repair.

At my previous home, a ranch in British Columbia, I built several mountain bluebird nesting boxes and fixed them, according to instructions, five feet from the ground, south-facing, on fence posts. I was proud when a pretty female bluebird took up residence. She started bringing in little sprigs of grass in her delicate beak to make a nest.

I bragged to my wife about my new tenant. I gloated to her about my important position as nature's aide. That is, until my wife beckoned me outside the following morning. I was horrified to see my wily old barn cat, Charlie, perched on the nesting box roof with a paw raised, ready to swat the unfortunate bird when she departed. I chased the cat away, evicted the little renter for her own good, and removed the box. Domestic cats tend to take full advantage of our generosity towards birds.

As cottagers, we tend to at least think we have a closer connection with nature, and we want to help out in any small way we can. We do things with all good intentions, to the best of our ability, and with all available information. Still, we can fail and discover that nature might have fared better without our intervention.

That is how I felt when I discovered the abandoned eggs. My wise, glass-half-full wife pointed out our successes, and the many young mergansers who began their lives in our little nesting box. Hopefully a talented young merganser mother will take up residence next spring, and when we see that young brood following their mother around the bay, we can be proud.

Time Moves On

I attended my oldest daughter's Grade 8 graduation during the last week of school. It was one of those bittersweet moments. As she received her diploma, wobbling across the stage in high heels that proved themselves far more difficult than the usual runners or flip-flops, I beamed with a father's pride. My little girl had grown up.

At the same time, I took in the ceremony with a somewhat heavy heart. Sure she had grown, but how fleeting those childhood days seem now. Was it not just yesterday that I carried her around on my shoulders and bounced her on my knee? She walked in my footsteps. I was her hero and she was my princess — well, no, she was never a princess. Now, she worries that I may embarrass her — and I undoubtedly have by even mentioning her in this space.

Time moves on and she has grown up, and for this special night at least, she has traded her jeans, T-shirt, and sneakers for an elegant dress. I looked at her, and it frightened me. She was beautiful. My daughter was no longer a child, she was a woman, and I was in trouble. I looked around

Life moves on and you can't change that.

me, and I am sure this is a sentiment most of the parents shared when seeing their daughters and sons maturing like this.

When I said that I would like to get her a graduation present, she suggested a cellphone, something that many of her friends have received. I considered it for a moment and then bought her a kayak. I think she was quite pleased with the surprise, and if she is anything like me, she does not really like talking on a phone anyway.

So, with the school year behind us, we head to the cottage with our graduate's new toy strapped to the car roof. She quickly catches on to the movement and rhythm of the craft. When she rises in the morning, she takes it out into the little bay in front of the cottage and paddles effortlessly around in circles and figure eights. She paddles around the island. Her strokes are smooth and powerful. She becomes more proficient, so the paddle seems to become an extension of her arms and the kayak becomes part of her lower body. The movement is elegant and silent, and I realize why many people get addicted to such travel.

When I brought a good report home in Grade 1, my dad built me a little wooden paddleboat called Flipper, named after the television series about a dolphin. Flipper was like a surfboard that you sat on and propelled yourself along with a double-bladed paddle. I enjoyed exploring on my little boat. Flipper is still around, but is used now as a bench in the children's fort.

I love sitting on the dock in the morning with my coffee, watching the kayak glide quietly across the water. My oldest will be off to high school in the fall. I know time passes quickly and soon she will be getting a summer job, graduating from high school, and perhaps leaving for university. Friends and commitments will lessen her time at the cottage. I don't look forward to those days. I like having the whole family here with me. But such is life, and it will happen to each of my children in turn, just as it happened to me and my parents. Life moves on, and you can't change that.

For now I'll enjoy watching a young lady and her kayak — and I'm happy that cellphones don't work out here.

Summertime Escape

Leave It to Beaver

A friend of mine was attacked by a beaver. Now, don't laugh, it's true. He told us so himself. We were at the cottage and there were a few of us, outdoor types, sitting around the campfire exchanging bear stories, when he joins in to tell us how he was nearly mauled by this plump rodent. You can imagine our mirth at his little yarn — we all shared a good laugh. He was serious, though, and visibly shaken recalling the experience.

This friend is a forestry worker, a consultant. As such, he spends much of his time in the outdoors. He is in the bush through all seasons and in any weather, sunshine, rain, and snow. Until the time of the attack, his only worries were the occasional black bear, and the blackflies and mosquitoes that torment him each spring.

He has a dog that accompanies him on his wilderness treks, a Siberian husky that loves the outdoors, the adventure, and the exercise. Well, not too long ago, as he was busy working in the bush, our friend heard the dog barking nearby. Now, huskies are not natural barkers, so he deemed the disturbance worth investigating.

He found the dog facing off with a rather large beaver — the beaver was confidently eyeing the canine. Fearing for the beaver's well-being, this caring forestry worker called off his well-behaved husky and ordered it to stay at a distance. He was fascinated to see this beaver so far from any water. There was no pond, lake, or river in the near vicinity. As he was admiring the pluck of the adventurous mammal, he was shocked to find himself under attack.

The beaver charged, and our poor friend was quickly backpedalling. The awkward-looking attacker darted in with more speed than seemed possible. Our hero dipped and dodged, weaved and wobbled, until he found himself with his back to a tree. The beaver gnashed his large front teeth. It seemed like curtains for our friend, but like a well-written movie, he found a large stick lying by his right hand. Just in the nick of time, he stuck out the broken branch and held the ferocious creature at bay.

The beaver backed off a little, and, seizing the opportunity, our brave forester sprinted off. He did not look behind him, did not worry about his dog, did not stop until he had reached the safety of his truck. You can imagine how we laughed when we heard this campfire tale, giggled until our bellies hurt. I feel sorry for laughing now.

I have shared my friend's scary account with others around the lake, and in turn have been given several similar stories of suspense involving the ferocious flat-tailed tree-eater. One poor fellow required stitches in his backside. A beaver had blocked his way over a bridge. He left the safety of his vehicle to gently shoo the cute critter from his path. The beaver charged, and the man turned and ran. The fleet-footed furball caught him, pinning the man between truck and bridge guard rail as he struggled to open his door. The beaver latched on to the startled victim's posterior, gnawing on it like it was a poplar tree.

An old rancher friend from the west told me of his own experience. When out riding his horse, repairing fence, he caught site of a beaver far from any pond. Before the cowboy could spit a tobacco plug, the creature had lunged at his mount's front legs. The beaver put the run on the horse in such an expert fashion that the cowpoke considered training the agile rodent for cutting cattle.

Now, we all have our cottage stories of *Castor canadensis* — of the damage they cause, the trees they thin, the marsh systems they help create, or simply the sound of their wide tails smacking water on a still summer's night. What has put me in mind of these violent tales is that today, as I am writing this, it is Canada Day, a day when we salute our country and feel pride for our flag. It is true we often complain that, as national symbols, the Americans have their bald eagle, the Russians their fearsome bear, and the Brits their king of the beasts, the lion. We have our amphibious rodent. Though these bucktoothed engineers may be industrious, hard-working, and skilled, they have never been credited as ferocious warriors.

"Well, now you know the rest of the story."

It is so quiet and peaceful here — it seems as if you have the world all to yourself.

First Job

My first job was for $1.25 an hour, cutting the extensive grass around the resort at the end of our lake. I would whack the high weeds along the lakeshore with a curved metal scythe and manhandle the smoky, belching gas mower over the unruly lawn that surrounded the wood cabins.

Sometimes I would shred some bramble with the mower blades and cut into a hornets' nest. The boss would laugh at the sight of me sprinting up the gravel laneway. When there was not much wind, the blackflies and mosquitoes would buzz around my head, landing in the sweat streams that flowed from my stringy hair. Hey, this was the seventies, and I had a mullet. What can I say? I had just turned fifteen years of age, and this was the dream job, away from town, close to the cottage.

At noon I would sit on the steep shoreline eating my bagged lunch, all the while looking over with envy at our island. I could see my siblings and cousins running wild, chasing each other through the trees, following their imaginations. In the heat of the afternoon, as I put fibreglass patches on old rental canoes, I saw the gang out with the boat water-skiing. They skied in circles and figure eights, and when they came close to the mainland they would wave at me. I would wave back.

They envied me for my work and the money I was making. I envied them their freedom. If I stared out too long the boss would yell down to me, "Done those canoes yet? If you'd rather be over there playing, you best go, I'm not paying you to daydream."

I spent the summer staining cabins and painting trim, moving rocks and splitting and stacking wood. When boats sidled up to the dock, I would stop what I was doing, run down, and top up their tanks. They would ask me if I was one of the Ross boys from the island. They would tell me about where the fish were biting on the lake. They would warn me of the big storm that would hit the next day. I would take the information home, and sometimes it would be right.

When people wandered into the little confectionery store, I would act as clerk or cashier. Sometimes I would exchange a couple of hours of work for some ice cream bars for my family at the cottage.

At five o'clock quitting time, as I stored the metal weed whacker and the ancient lawn mower, I would see our boat leave the dock and head my way. It was a great feeling, the end of the workday. I would get back to the cabin and throw on my swim shorts — wash off the day's dust and grime in the lake. Dad would take me for a spin on the skis. Mom would clang the dinner bell.

I remember it as a summer when I was leaving my childhood days behind. After a five-day workweek, I would be given fifty dollars. I had never seen so much money. My wages went to a new slalom ski from Canadian Tire, bright orange with a yellow dragon. It still hangs in the boathouse today, and when I take it down and see the cracking and rotting thick rubber footholds, feel the scratches and chips that are a testament to years of use, memories of my first job, and an amazing summer, come flooding back.

The Perfect Storm

The day had been hot and humid. The lake had been calm. We enjoyed some swimming and skiing, and now, at dusk, we light a driftwood fire on the rocky point.

Before we see the sky darkening up the north arm, we feel the weather changing. It seeps into your senses, and your mind tells you that the last time you felt this way, a storm was coming. Not to let you feel too good about your instincts, however, you realize that it was an hour ago that you noticed the loons calling each other in a frantic way; now they have disappeared. Your dogs snuck quietly away from the bonfire and have undoubtedly crawled under the porch. Only the gulls play in the approaching blow, riding high on the wind and then arcing back low over the water.

The wind quickens with shocking speed. It blows the water into a rugged chop, whitecaps curl over, and trees begin to bend. Lightning at first lights the distant sky like small explosions. As it moves down the lake, you can see the jagged forks touch the water. The storm gets closer. Waves crash into the rocky shoreline. A lone fishing boat motors quickly for shore.

We douse the fire with our bucket, although I am certain that the coming rain would do the job for us, and then we gather up everything and head for the cabin. Towels are pulled from the clothesline and thrown into a basket. The children secure their toys and tubes, and I make sure that the boat is covered and made tight to the dock. The wind howls through with more velocity, so we have to shout to hear each other. I tie down the canvas door of the kid's wall tent. The flag flaps noisily.

We light the propane lights and oil lanterns in the cabin, and the children pull out a deck of cards. I sit outside under the covered porch; the howling wind and rolling waves leave me feeling serene. The rain hits suddenly; it does not start slowly but gets thrown down. Horizontal drops pelt the cottage

Here at the cottage, a storm brings a wild and astonishing beauty.

windows and buffet me under the porch roof — so I sneak inside, and we all gather to watch the show from the big front window. Thunder shakes the cabin, and the kids scream with excitement. They count aloud the seconds between thunder and lightning. Boom and bolt happen simultaneously, and prongs of lightning seem to strike into our little bay.

My wife asks me to go out to see if the dogs are all right. She thinks she has heard the crash of a tree as it hit the privy. She wonders aloud whether the swim raft has broken its moorings and floated to the far end of the lake. She thinks I should go check on the boat. I watch the lightning touch down nearby, and wonder whether getting life insurance with her encouragement was such a good idea.

The storm rages for about an hour, and then the clouds move off to the south, the sound and light disappear over the distant hills. The lake calms perceptibly, and the stars come out. Still, the children decide they will sleep in the loft rather than the tent tonight. I wander around to check on things. The island smells damp and cool. Besides some broken branches and boughs, all is well.

I love a good storm. I recall being caught outside in many. I remember canoe trips, scrambling to get tents set up when a squall hits, and mountain storms on horse pack trips, trying to get horses fed while the wind whips your long slicker and rain streams from your hat. Nothing beats a cottage storm, when you are warm and cozy, under the soft glow of the oil lamps with a fire burning in the wood stove, looking out at the sound and fury over the lake.

At home, a storm like this would have brought worries of power outages, surges, driving problems. Here at the cottage, it just brings a wild and astonishing beauty ... the perfect storm.

Holding the Fort

Some stories are better started at the end.

My wife, sister, and brother-in-law, back from a shopping expedition, came walking into a cottage thick with smoke. The cabin was a disaster.

There I stood, my pants soaked in an area that suggested I had wet myself, hot dogs smeared into my jeans and scattered about my feet, the charred remains of something inedible visible on the oven rack behind the open stove door, and my shirt ripped and tattered and scorched black. On my face was a smile that probably looked quite idiotic — but it was simply meant to calm the horrified expressions that greeted me and to convey the message that all was okay and you won't believe this.

Their worry was not for my predicament, however, which became evident when the ladies asked loudly in unison, "Are the kids all right?"

"Oh, yes." I had forgotten about them.

"Where are they?"

"Oh — they're out there." I made a sweeping gesture with my hand, indicating a wide radius where the children might be found. "They're on the island — somewhere …"

My wife gave me a practised glower. My sister shook her head disbelievingly. My brother-in-law smiled — he had one-upped me in the constant understated competition of looking good to the spouses.

Now, perhaps it's best if I go back to the beginning.

My sister has always thought me totally inept in all things responsible and domestic. It was with a countenance of worry that she had begrudgingly agreed to leave me in charge of our combined seven children, while the three mature adults headed to town to restock our provisions.

"Don't let them play too close to the water. Don't let them play with the axe or the chainsaw. Don't let them play with matches. Don't encourage them to swim to shore." And then to her oldest boy the heartfelt plea — "Watch over your brothers and cousins, please."

In their absence, I was determined to prove my sister's lack of confidence misplaced. I went back to my work, sealing the cracks between logs and around window and door frames, but diligently, on the quarter hour, I hollered out into the thick forest asking if all was well. Each time, the response was affirmative. On the occasion of my fifteenth check, I received the response, "What's for lunch?"

"Hot dogs!" I bellowed, wanting to sound like I had a plan.

So back to the cabin I went, lit the propane oven, and tossed in a dozen buns. I placed a pot full of wieners and water on the gas element, then flicked my butane igniter — poof, easy. I hung up the lighter, very pleased with myself. I felt my stomach getting quite warm. I looked down, and to my horror saw that my paint-stained, soiled work shirt was afire. I patted it gingerly with my open palm, which made a "whoosh, whoosh" sound as it fanned the flame. Now, I knew what I was supposed to do in an emergency like this, but I was alone in a cottage far from civilization, and I would have felt quite silly rolling around with this small flame burning on my belly. So I waved my hand harder, which served to both spread the fire and knock the pot of wieners and water from their stovetop perch — water unfortunately soaking my pants but avoiding the fire.

I rolled on the ground. I wasn't burnt, but it was a mess. Then I heard the boat docking. I panicked and looked for the broom — seeing instead black smoke billowing out of the oven.

Now, in this, the last chance I will ever be afforded to "hold the fort," I did learn a lesson. The spray-in foam insulation is very flammable before it cures. So, if you've been working with it, guys, and wiping your hands on your work shirts, be very careful to not burn your wieners.

Death of a Dog

Unfortunately, I have buried many dogs in my lifetime — such is the canine business that I am in. But the one who lies beneath a stand of old cedars on our island's highest point was the first to be laid to rest at the cottage.

The day before had been like any other at the lake. The sun was warm, and we had spent the day playing in and on the water. The dog had run his usual distances, watching over the children in their play, keeping his eye on us, making sure to miss nothing and that nothing was amiss.

Macky was not only a pet, but also a sled dog and my leader. He had worked by my side for years, helping me to earn my living. When his winter work was over, his happiest days were when he saw us loading up the truck with paddles and life jackets, propane tanks and fishing rods — criteria for him that signalled a trip to the cottage. He loved coming to the island because it meant a world of freedom, a place surrounded by water where he could run to his heart's content. Nothing ever escaped his attention, especially if it smelt of trouble or adventure.

When I woke from the boathouse bunkie in the morning, Macky was not there to greet me, as was his usual custom. I found him sick and distraught, lying under the boughs of an old spruce. He groaned. His stomach was rock hard.

The day was dark and stormy. Thunder bellowed from the west and sheets of lightning lit the water. I picked up the dog and ran for the boat. The remoteness that was a desired part of our cottage escape was suddenly an enemy, and the drive to town was long. We made it to the vet in time to see the dog's last breath, and I knew that if this had not happened at the cottage, perhaps we could have prolonged his life.

Death had joined Mack to the placed he loved.

I wept gently as I dug the hole for Macky, hacking away at tree roots and prying out rocks until it was sufficiently deep. I laid the dog's muscular, handsome black and white body inside, tucked in his enormous paws, and used his old sleeping blanket as a shroud. On my hands and knees, I packed in the damp, spongy brown soil with a flat-faced shovel, pushing it down until the hole was full, swollen with its new burden. Then I marked the grave with a flat piece of granite I pulled from the lake.

When this was done, my children joined me looking down at the mounded earth. My oldest cried with me, as we both knew we would never again see this old dog running wild at our cottage. My youngest, not fully understanding, tilted her head back and looked up at me, concerned for my tears. She thought it was only she who wept.

We don't know what happened. Perhaps he had eaten something he shouldn't have. Perhaps it was just his time. The old-timers on the lake gave their theories — poison toads, tainted mushrooms, reaction to a bee sting. What was indisputable was that he had lived well, a long and full life.

Though he may have managed to live slightly longer if we were home and closer to help, in the end death had joined Macky to the place he loved. We can all wish for a similar end.

First Ski

Learning to water-ski is a little bit like learning to ride a bicycle. Okay, so one of them is on dry land and one is in the water, one of them is on two wheels and the other is on two boards. Still, it is balance and trying, and falling and trying again, and skinning your knee or swallowing lake water, and then trying one more time.

With training wheels off, you hold the seat of your kid's bike and run along behind. You let go for a second and the bike starts to wobble, so you lunge forward, grab on, and run some more. You might just be getting into the best shape of your life. Finally, on the umpteenth try, you let go and the child just pedals away. You jog a bit further, but you know the time has come. You stop and try to cheer, but you are wheezing, hunched over, and gasping for breath. So you delicately give a thumbs-up.

My nine-year-old son got up on water skis this week. He has been working hard at it this summer, trying to keep up with his older sisters. We do not have the fancy training bars on the boat, or any particular model of learning skis. When the children's feet fit into the smallest pair of water skis we own, they are welcome to give it a try.

They get into the water, hold the rope, yell "Hit it," and then we see where it takes us. We get into the water with them, hold them steady, bombard them with little tidbits of useless advice, and then watch helplessly as they are jerked quickly to the surface of the water. Just as quickly, they get tossed back into the lake with a violent splash and a clatter of skis. Their legs go in different directions, so you are sure their limber bodies will be torn in two.

We swim up to them and tell them that they were almost up. We urge them to give it another try. "Don't let go so quickly," we tell them. They trust us and try again — this time hanging on to the tow bar far too long after they have fallen, dragging themselves through the water like a torpedo, swallowing half of the lake. "Just about," we yell when they finally surface.

I do not think any of us really know what the secret to getting up on the skis is — at least I know I don't. We give advice culled from our years of skiing, but until everything comes together for them, in their own brains, they are going nowhere.

Then the time comes. He is up — unsteady, yes, but up and skiing. His skis drift apart, and with body language you try to will him out of the splits. He bends too far forward and bobs over some rough water, but refuses to go down. The wide smile on his face is reward enough for all the patience and repetition. You try to cheer, but instead take in a mouthful of lake water and only sputter and cough and stick a thumbs-up. You realize you are freezing to death. You realize that the boat is coming back around and you're bobbing in the middle of the bay. You swim frantically for shore and realize that you were in better shape way back when you were teaching him to ride his bicycle.

It's all worth it, because he is skiing, and he is feeling good about himself. You know that now that he has gotten up, he will always get up, always be able to ski. Like learning to ride a bike, when you put it all together and rise out of the water ... there is no going back. You never seem to forget the secret, the secret that can be learned but never shared.

Like learning to ride a bike — when they put it all together and rise from the water, there is no going back.

He will open his eyes in the morning — the late morning — and look out at a lake as calm as glass, the perfect, still water for skiing. He will say, "Dad, can I go skiing?" You will put down your book and your coffee, drop whatever it is you are doing, and drag him around the lake. Sometimes you will ask yourself, Why did I ever teach him to do this? Mostly, you are just happy that you don't have to swim around for hours in the cool lake water anymore, helping him out. Well, until it comes time for your next one, the six-year-old, the youngest, to give it a go.

Life Is a Game

I am feeling very dejected this evening. I'm sitting at the kitchen table with my head in my hands, looking down at a mess of cards and a cribbage board, while my seven-year-old card shark of a daughter dances around the cottage chanting, "I skunked daddy!" It doesn't seem very long ago that we were teaching her the game and taking it easy on her while she learned. Now, I try my hardest, but … "I smell something skunky," she sings. "Is there a smell in the room?"

"It's a good game for learning her numbers, isn't it?" I grumble to my wife.

I don't know about you, but we play a lot of games with the whole family when we are at the cottage. Most evenings, after the supper dishes have been cleaned up, we will sit around the big kitchen table and pull out a game. Sometimes, when the rain clouds have closed in and it's wet and grey outside, we might spend an afternoon rolling dice and moving little men around a board. There is something about the cottage and the tradition of games.

Perhaps it is because we have no electricity at our island cabin, and therefore no television, video games, or any such diversions. I believe it is more than that, though. A trip to the cottage is a step back to simpler times, and those simpler times are more conducive to quality family time.

We have a storage bench where all the games are kept. Some have been there for thirty-some years, since I was a kid. Some are more modern. A couple are missing a piece or two, replaced by makeshift cards or odd trinkets. Some of the boxes have been taped up, while others are in mint condition.

We have original editions of Clue and Monopoly, two perennial favourites. There are Risk, Full House, Masterpiece, and Life. There are checkers and Chinese checkers, chess, backgammon, and Mastermind. We have an old Rummoli game where we can teach the children how to gamble, in the same manner and on the same board where I learned how to play poker with my parents when I was young. In my dad's handwriting on one corner of the board, now slightly faded and barely legible, is the order of what beats what, from royal flush down to ace high.

Of course, there are several decks of cards, most of them complete. We love a good round of euchre or hearts. There are modern games like The Settlers of Catan and Cranium. When bigger groups gather, we can make fools of ourselves playing Pictionary, Balderdash, Trivial Pursuit, or charades. My wife and I will sit on the dock on a quiet afternoon and play a game of Scrabble.

I remember my siblings and me cleaning up after supper while my parents went for an evening paddle. Then we would get a game set up and eagerly await their return. Playing a game with the parents was always something we looked forward to — it was a memorable part of cottage life.

Another memory is of my parents going to a friend's for dinner. They returned talking about all that happened in the evening, and I could hear them from my bed. I caught snippets of their conversation: some murdered body, hit over the head with a candlestick, in a ballroom. From what I could understand, there were secret passages between rooms — how cool is that in the imaginative mind of a five-year-old? My mother had been hanging out with some professor in a billiard room, but my dad didn't seem to mind, even when the academic turned out to be a killer. My dad seemed to have followed some sexpot named Scarlet around, and this did seem to annoy my mother. I thought, boy adults have fun: people murdered, and what a mansion their friends must have! A game called Clue had just been introduced to North America.

Now, we sit around the table staring covertly at our secret notes, going from room to room playing detective in a race to find out who murdered Mr. Body. I am always Colonel Mustard. At one time the kids had a good giggle when I would jabber away in a rendition of an old colonel's English accent. Now, they just roll their eyes.

When we are at home during the school year, we sometimes think that it would be nice to set aside one evening a week for a family game night. Great idea, but it just never happens. Life with children is too busy. They are on the go, or we have other places to be and more important things to do.

At the cottage there is always time, and sitting around the table with the whole family and an old board game remains a wonderful way to spend it.

*Never turn
your back on
your sister.*

Cottage Guests

It doesn't matter how well you know them, cottage guests will always change when they come to your summer abode. Typically, there are three main types. There are those who show up with a sporting goods store strapped to their SUVs. They have canoes or kayaks, water skis and wakeboards, fishing rods, snorkelling gear, and baseball gloves. These active guests are up every morning at 6:00 a.m., and don't stop all weekend. They energize you. They tire you out.

Then there are the guests who park their backsides in the sitting room or on the dock and act like they are visiting some swank, four-star, all-inclusive resort. They like to say things like, "My beer is empty," "I'm hungry, when is lunch usually served?" and "You should build yourself a little trolley — it would make it easier for you to bring down all those appetizers and drinks, and save you some trips." They are always on time for dinner, and afterwards, while you clean up, they take the canoe out for a romantic evening paddle. "You should try it," they say.

Finally, there are the guests who immediately fall in love with the place, constantly smiling and shaking their heads in wonder. They are immediately at ease and totally comfortable in their surroundings. They like to read, and they tend to enjoy the simple things in life. They also like to help out with cottage projects, daily chores, and in cooking meals. Meal preparation becomes a social, fun time, with everyone getting involved. Some will volunteer to take charge of a homemade pizza night or some ethnic-themed meal.

While these visitors quickly fall into the relaxation mode, the others remain nervous and fidgety, having had to leave their workplace technology behind. They are out of their comfort zones, without their cellphones, laptops, and BlackBerries. In fact, they do not know what else to use their hands for. You find them nervously pacing around the dock in the morning, stretching and flexing their thumbs. During the drive home they check every kilometre to see if they are "back in range," and when they miraculously re-enter this connected zone, they immediately fall silent, all their concentration focussed on their techno addictions.

The children also like to invite their own young friends to spend some time at the cottage. Some are bored — "There is nothing to do!" Translation: they miss their cellphones, computers, video games, and text messages. These might remain friends, but they are city friends. The kids seem to have an innate ability to recognize the friends who will fit in, use their imaginations, and join in the time-tested cottage activities. At their summer escape, they want to surround themselves with those who will unabashedly play their made-up games of manhunt, James Bond, capture the flag, and, after dark, the sinister murder game. They play old, traditional board games, and can spend whole days frolicking in the lake, never complaining that they're cold.

The best cottage guests? They create memories that make you laugh. They suddenly pull harmonicas out of their pockets at the evening campfire and entertain. Who knew they were musical? They have their own fun and funky fireside songs and games. They religiously rise in the early morning, jump into the lake, and scream like some phantom lake monsters. They get the kids up early and take them out fishing. A fellow cottage friend said she had a guest who would play the trombone every morning at the end of the dock while the sun was rising. Others will lie out on the swim rock at night, looking up at the stars and pointing out to the kids all the constellations.

There is always that brief moment of contemplation — before the dive.

The guests we invite to our cottage, good friends and family alike, are those that we care enough about to want to share our favourite place on earth. The good ones do not simply take from the experience, but rather add to it. By doing so, they tend to find their way into our cottage lore. Also, by doing so, they tend to ensure themselves of another invite!

The Food Chain

My wife stumbled onto the battle scene first. She had gone to retrieve the watering can, which is stored under the front porch of the cottage, when she jumped back with a shrill screech.

Of course this drew the attention of my children, who, although they never seem to hear the clang of the dinner bell calling them for a meal, respond at once to a horrified yelp. They arrived at the scene even before I bravely came running to the rescue. We peered under the wood decking, crouching cautiously to gain a better view.

A long black, green, and yellow garter snake was the reason for my wife's consternation, but it was the battle that was ensuing that caught the fancy of the rest of us. There was a tug-of-war going on between the snake and a huge, brown, wrinkly toad. The snake had one of the toad's legs in its hinged mouth and was working hard to envelop the rest of the poor creature — a feat that seemed to me to be impossible.

In a fatherly way, I was a little concerned to have the children take in this morbid scene. The kids simply found the whole thing captivating — although the descriptive words "gross" and "sick" were generously applied. We watched as the snake gained some ground, pulling the toad farther under the wooden porch. Then we watched the toad hop gamely towards the light.

The battle continued for much of the day, and for most of the length of the deck. Though I lost interest after a time and returned to my work, the children exhibited an untiring fascination. They peered through the cracks and gave a running commentary. They cheered for the toad. When I shuffled them off into the cabin for bed that night, the battle had not yet been won — or lost.

The children were up unusually early the next day and quickly out to the covered porch, but after searching exhaustively and peering through every crack, they reported that the fight must have ended. They concluded that the toad must have escaped.

Later that same day, I came across the snake sunning itself on a rock by the water's edge. Evidence dictated that the battle's outcome had been very different from what my kids had hoped for, or I had thought possible. As the snake slithered slowly away, I could see the huge bulge halfway along the length of its sleek body. It looked like I feel after a huge Thanksgiving dinner.

Old-fashioned fun — shooting pebbles into the lake.

I wondered whether to tell the family about my find. I decided it best, for why hide nature's truths? I have seen a lot of things, but this was a lesson for me as well. I never thought it possible for this snake to swallow a toad the size of a softball.

And the lesson was not over. Not long after, as we were enjoying lunch on the dock, we saw our friendly red-tailed hawk wing past with what looked like a length of rope dangling from its talons.

The snake, made lazy and careless in victory, had become the victim. Another of nature's battles had been won and lost.

Island Kingdom

It is a beautiful sunny day. Wispy clouds drift lazily across the blue. My wife snoozes in the lounger with an open book on her lap. The children play on the swim raft moored in the bay, pushing each other off in some form of "king of the castle." The giggling and laughter is a beautiful sound. King of the raft they may be, but I am the monarch of this island, methinks, as I stand surveying my kingdom.

Often when we think of an earthly paradise, it is an island that is imagined. True, it is mostly a tropical destination, with white sand beaches, blue ocean, and swaying palms, but also it seems to be the self-containment that the island promises that is an important part of the fantasy.

My cottage is on an island. It is far from tropical; in fact, it can be quite chilly some days, even in summer. There is no sandy beach, no salty ocean air or turquoise water, no palms, sea birds, or tropical fish. The island is a balsam-scented, three-acre mound of rock, cedar, and pine situated in the middle of a lake in the northern woods. It is the island from a Tom Thomson painting. The conifers are bent in the wind and gnarled with age.

On the island, in a setting of white birch and mountain ash, is a rambling log cabin with a loft and ladder, polished wood furniture, a wood-burning fireplace, covered porch, and cedar privy. Muskoka chairs are on the dock at the end of a short, well-worn path. There is no electricity, telephone, or running water. A propane oven or little wood stove is where we do our cooking, and oil lamps help light the cabin at night. It is a relaxing place, and a fun and safe place for the family. The children and our dogs can run around and we do not worry. The island provides a combination of freedom and security.

The island might lack the tropical flavour or even the fearsome cliffs or craggy mountains that fix some islands in one's memory. Here, at the cottage, the beauty is more modest than spectacular. It is beautiful, though, surrounded by inviting water and a sweeping panorama of inlets, islands, and peninsulas.

King of the castle — giggling and laughter are beautiful sounds.

True, cottaging on a remote island can provide certain obstacles. One cannot so readily hop in the car and head to town for milk and bread. It is a little bit more of a logistical dilemma when everything has to be brought by boat — the provisions for a week's stay, the hundred-pound propane cylinders needed for cooking and refrigeration, or the lumber for a cottage project. The marvellous sense of isolation is peculiar to islands, and it is this isolation that both limits distractions and demands self-sufficiency.

I have always thought of myself as an island person. My wife and family would say that I am frugal. I am self-sufficient, comfortable with solitude, an avid reader, and greedy for small pleasures. Since this is an island that has been in the family since my childhood, the cottage also encourages a powerful nostalgia in me.

It was on the island that I learned to fish and canoe, water-ski, chop wood — it was here that I grew to manhood. I cut a deep, jagged gash in my left pointer finger when the crosscut saw I was using slipped out of the log. I hid by the water on a rock ledge surrounded by cedars, not wanting to admit my careless mistake — holding a blood-soaked cloth over a wound that needed stitches. Unembarrassed now, I show the scar to my children.

Yes, back then I was just a kid, a mere serf in this domain. Now I am royalty!

The children are at the shore now, climbing out on swim rock, asking what is for lunch. My wife is awake, giving me orders to put the barbecue on for hot dogs.

"Can you take us out water-skiing after lunch?" the kids ask.

"You said you'd take me fishing," my son reminds me.

"And you were going to fix the dock this afternoon," suggests my wife.

"Yes, my liege," says the man who would be king.

Puppy Love

I recently introduced a new family pet to life at the cottage. Boomer is a year-old husky, playful, athletic, good-looking, and a little thick. Technically he is no longer a puppy, though he certainly does act like one.

It was love at first sight for him as far as the cottage goes. And why not? Cottage life is a perfect fit for most dogs. Upon arrival on the three-acre island he is in constant motion. There are so many new sights, smells, and places to explore. As we unpack and get things organized, Boomer and Timba run this way and that. They are just two medium-sized huskies, but sound like a whole herd of elephants as they thunder past.

With my chores complete, I sit down in the rocker on the front porch and open an ice-cold beverage. I'm asked to light the barbecue, so I set down the beer for just a second and step off the porch. When I turn back I see that the darling pup has pierced the tin with his incisors and is lapping up the spraying liquid. I let out a piercing scream, causing Boomer to dart off into the trees with the can of Kilkenny still clenched in his teeth. It's my own fault. Why would I leave an almost full tin of cold, crisp ale unguarded? Who could blame the parched canine, overheated from all the running, for satisfying his thirst.

After dinner I take the kids for a quick ski. Boomer worries greatly about this ritual, people being dragged around the water on a rope, kind of like backwards dog sledding. He paces and whines, and smooches with the children when they return safely to the dock. At one point he leans out too far and tumbles into the lake. He panics and swims under the dock and gets stuck there looking like a drowned rat. I have to get in the water and rescue him.

We take an evening paddle around the island. Boomer follows us on land, dashing around the trail, alighting on different rocky viewpoints on the shore. When we pass that point, he darts back into the bush and reappears at the next rocky precipice. When we return to the dock, he comes bounding down, slips and slides off and into the water. He tries to swim underneath the stringers and gets stuck. I look at Timba and we both shake our heads.

I had a restless sleep in the boathouse bunkie that night, as I tossed and turned and dreamt about being on an African safari with elephants, lions, and hyenas circling my tent. The night is filled with all kinds of weird African noises. In a sleepy, half-dazed, early-morning state I stumble to the cabin to put on some coffee, and almost immediately fall into a huge crater that was dug in the middle of the trail. I yell for help, but neither human nor dog responds, so I scramble out of the hole myself. It appears that the dog had been trying to dig up some kind of rodent, perhaps a vole.

She would welcome the kids back to land — swimming and skiing, were to her, supreme acts of folly.

Awake now, I look at the scene before me, horrified. It looks like a war zone, even worse than the kids' bedrooms at home. Somehow Boomer has opened the door to the utility shed and dragged everything out — tools, nails, gas cans, boat oil, pieces of lumber, paintbrushes, tarps, and rope. Every knick-knack necessary for cottage survival is spread about. He has even pulled out the chainsaw and appears to have tried to start it.

I then find all the cooking utensils that usually hang neatly on the barbecue, scattered about like there has been some wild doggy party. The metal tongs and spatula are dinted and dimpled with teeth marks. The handle of the cleaning brush has been eaten off.

I find bits of clothing that had been left outside. Some of it is still recognizable. The dog grabbed my oldest daughter's bikini bottoms, although I would have thought he would rather sink his teeth into something a little more substantial, and chewed them even smaller, thong size. My comfortable sneakers have been transformed into thongs of a different sort. A bottle of sun block has been squeezed empty, spread over the cottage wall. I'm not sure, but it looks as if he was spelling his name.

I find Boomer sleeping on the deck, with an air of innocence. The truth being, he had nothing left to chew. Timba sits beside him looking mortified. When I throw her a questioning look, she shakes her head and lifts a paw, pointing it at the snoozing pup.

"Boomer!" I yell angrily. He bounds to his feet with tail wagging wildly, jumps up on me and starts licking my face. He seems to be telling me, "I love this place!"

Lost in Translation

Grandma and six-year-old Jenna saw the one-legged duck coming out of the bay. It hopped quite ably up onto the shore and grazed in the long grass that fringed the water. It had learned to lean over to the right, to balance itself and compensate for the loss of the left leg.

How it lost its appendage, we do not know. The children would later guess at a snapping turtle, a pike, or perhaps a crazed boater. Maybe it was a dog. The duck might have lost it as a duckling. He might have been born with only one leg. We can only guess. The reality was that the whole leg was missing, but he had learned to cope. Not just to cope, but to manoeuvre himself around on the grass with a dexterity that was very impressive.

Grandma had not seen this duck before, so she sent Jenna scurrying up to the cottage to fetch Grandpa, to tell him to come down and see.

"Is Grandpa coming?" asked Grandma, when the youngster returned.

"No, he's already seen it," answered Jenna, sitting herself back down.

"Really? He never told me," said Grandma, a little miffed.

*There's
a certain
simplicity to life
at the cottage.*

"He said he saw it yesterday, he saw the leg fall off in the water."

Jenna was quite matter-of-fact about what Grandpa had seen. Grandma was a little harder to convince. "What? Grandpa said that? He saw the duck's leg fall off?" Jenna smiled and nodded; Grandma looked up towards the cottage in disbelief.

"He said he saw the leg fall right off when the water was high — he knows where he can find it," stated young Jenna. Grandma envisioned herself packing the thin duck leg in a bag of ice and rushing off with the leg and bird to the nearest hospital to have it sewn back on.

Completely ambivalent that he was at the centre of what might become a domestic dispute, the one-legged duck hopped gamely back down into the water and floated gracefully away, through the reeds and out of sight.

Grandpa came down with a tray, some sandwiches, and drinks. Now, he has been married to Grandma for fifty years and can easily recognize the signs of danger. He was in trouble, but he had no idea why. So he did what brave men everywhere do when faced with the wrath of their spouses: he pleaded innocence even before being accused.

"What? I didn't do anything," he said — hands out to his sides, palms upward.

"You never told me you saw a one-legged duck," chastised Grandma. Grandpa looked around the shore and out in the bay. "Well, he's gone now! And why did you tell Jenna you saw its leg drop off?"

"I said no such thing," harrumphed Grandpa.

"You said that, Grandpa," accused the innocent young girl, sidling up to Grandma, knowing at a young age that women should stick together. "You said you saw the leg fall right off the duck."

Grandpa stood open-mouthed, speechless. He looked at Jenna, and then at Grandma — both had their arms crossed and were glaring at him. Then he thought of something, and he smiled; all was becoming clear. This was all about a six-year-old's pronunciation, and the hearing of a grandparent.

"The dock — I saw the pin drop out of the dock." The ramp from shore to their floating dock sat at a peculiar angle. The water level had risen the day before, lifting the dock and causing the pin to fall off into the shallow waters. "I thought Jenna was telling me about the dock — I saw the leg fall off the dock."

Grandpa has yet to see the amazing one-legged duck … the little troublemaker.

The Handyman

I'm not a handyman. I admit it. Even my kids recognize this. When a cottage project comes along that requires a little more of a craftsman's touch, they say, "Better get Grandpa." When I tell them that I think I can do this, they say, "Dad, stick to building fences and docks." My wife, bless her heart, has a certain confidence in my carpentry skills. Either that, or she loves to see me make a fool of myself.

I know this, because whenever a new issue of the magazine *Cottage Life* arrives, I have to try to be the one to retrieve the mail. This way I can flip through the magazine and tear out any puttering, inventive, handyman projects that might catch her fancy. She'll say, "We seem to be missing pages 94 to 102."

To which I'll shake my head and respond, "You really don't know how magazines work, do you? They always keep a few pages in reserve in case a late, great story is submitted."

Unfortunately, there are those times when I have to work and cannot hang around the mailbox all day. I get home and there she will be, leafing through the pages of the latest issue. "Oh," she says, "you should come and see this. Think we [meaning you] can build it?"

So I try to build a bar trolley to wheel down to the dock. The wheels fall off on its first mission, and we lose half of our cocktail supply. Who knew you couldn't just nail the wheels on? Then I build the fancy, floating dumb waiter to get drinks and lunch out to the swim raft. It sinks.

In the latest "Special Anniversary" August 2007 issue, there is a six-and-a-half-page spread, complete with photography and illustrations, describing the building of a two-seater wooden Muskoka loveseat that doubles, mysteriously, as a canoe rack. Not only a canoe rack, but also a canoe lift — it helps you hoist your canoe out of the water. I notice that my wife has dog-eared the page. What a dumb idea. Whatever happened to the days when you would canoe to the dock, reach down, grab the gunnel, hoist the canoe over your head, and carry it to the canoe rack on shore?

"We [meaning you] should build one of these." She sees it as a romantic loveseat — that it is also a canoe hoist is of no consequence.

"But you could only sit in the chair if I was out paddling the canoe," I whine.

"Exactly!"

I imagine myself paddling the canoe around the island, around the bay, pleading with her to let me dock for lunch. "Just a few more minutes," she will say, "I just want to finish this chapter."

Worse, I envision her sitting and flirting in the loveseat with Hunk Hankinson, the real handyman on the lake, who lives in the fancy, overbuilt, over-organized cottage on shore. I would be out paddling, and paddling some more, waiting for permission from my controller to begin my approach and land. Meanwhile, he would be pointing out all the flaws in my creation, telling her how he would have done it better, and they would both be giggling. I might be allowed brief docking privileges if their drinks were to run dry.

All this for a silly loveseat that transforms itself into a canoe hoist and rack. I see myself sidling up to the dock in my canoe, hopping out, tying off, going around and flipping the hinged seat over and into the canoe, and then going back to the canoe to line it up with the overturned seat and to attach the chair armrests to the canoe thwarts. Then, getting back on the dock, I would untie the canoe from the dock cleats, before going around and pulling on the hoisting ropes to flip both the chair and canoe over and onto the dock. The half-hour process complete, my wife would wander down with her book and a sandwich and say, "Hey, I was just about to sit in that chair!"

The Cottage Duel

Okay, it's not really the same as pistols at fifty paces, a good old medieval joust, or a bare-knuckled boxing match in the school playground, but, at the cottage, it is a fair means of settling disputes. Insults have been cast, a challenge is made and accepted, and the duel begins. The combat sometimes lasts for only a few brief seconds. Other battles can take fifteen minutes or more. The winner stays dry. The loser suffers an embarrassing dunking in the lake.

We call it gunnel bobbing, a canoe-based balancing act akin to lumberjack log rolling. The two combatants paddle out into the bay, one climbs up on the stern, the other on the bow, both face each other with feet firmly planted on the canoe gunnels. The idea is to shake and bob and wobble the canoe around to throw your opponent off balance. When you see you're getting the upper hand, you go for the kill — a couple of hard shakes has them tumbling into the surf.

For us, gunnel bobbing had become a somewhat forgotten sport. Canoes were used for more practical purposes, like paddling around on a quiet evening or heading out on a multi-day trip. We were going through an old box of snapshots, which we had discovered stored away at the back of a cupboard at the cottage, when we came across some goofy photos of us as kids, gunnel bobbing out in the little bay on my brother's cedar strip canoe. After commenting on the horrendous styles of our circa 1979 bathing trunks and bikinis, our kids were excited to have discovered another way to have fun at the cabin. A tournament was arranged: it would be sister against sister, sister against brother, and cousin against cousin. The "All World Cottage Gunnel Bobbing Championship" was at stake.

My past experience made me resident expert, coach, trainer, and judge. When coaching new combatants, I always stress the point that it is unwise to try to hang on when a dunking is inevitable. Refusing to face certain defeat usually just means that you tumble into the canoe instead of into the refreshing water. That can hurt — so, when you are losing your balance, the best strategy is to jump clear into the lake.

It is a lesson that stubborn boys, in particular, are slow to learn. This is especially so when they are paired with their obnoxious sisters: they must win at all costs. So it is with my son's first competition. He does what I warned against and topples into the canoe upon losing his balance — one leg in the boat and one in the lake, his tender acorns cracking on the canoe gunnel. Boys, of course, hate to smack their nether-regions, while at the same time they get a kind of perverse giggly pleasure out of falling in such an uncomfortable manner. All onlookers of the male variety groan and grimace and hunch over in discomfort when bearing witness to such a tragedy. With his pale face contorted in instant agony, my son teeters slow-motion overboard and into the lake. The cool water obviously plays a hand in hurrying his recovery.

In the end, one of the male cousins is crowned champion. With this knowledge, I unwittingly extol the virtues of the male athlete as superior to that of the fairer sex. I, too, I point out, was a hero in my day. Having heard enough, my wife challenges me to a duel.

My superior cunning, athleticism, and balance pays off (as well as the fact that I start the battle before she says "Go!"). I thus have her scrambling to find a foothold from the beginning, and in no time at all she tumbles into the cool lake water. Victory is mine. I am the greatest! Unfortunately, when you are a little heavier, even when you win the battle, you lose. As soon as I have managed to rid myself of the bow ballast, my weight in the stern throws the bow of the canoe high in the air, so that the sixteen-foot prospector looks more like a rocket ready for lift-off than a canoe ready to be paddled to shore. I feel immediately like the captain of the *Titanic*, and prepare to go down with the ship, joining my grumpy wife in the lake.

Such is life, and a hard lesson for me, and for men, everywhere to learn. The rest of the evening is spent in relative silence. Supper is a fend for

It's not pistols at fifty paces, a medieval joust, or a playground boxing match, but at the cottage it's a fair way of settling disputes.

yourself, as my darling spouse has decided she is not hungry. All my peace offerings are rebuked. Life is a bit like gunnel bobbing. Sometimes you are better off just taking the fall, because often even when you win, you lose.

A Gathering of Loons

Come here, Norman ... hurry up. The loons! The loons!
They're welcoming us back.
  — Ethel Thayer in Ernest Thompson's *On Golden Pond*

We heard the first two loons flying overhead before we saw them settling on the lake. They were soon joined by our resident couple, as the duo that frequented our little bay floated in, hooting softly. I was about to head back to the cabin when I saw a third pair winging in from the north. The four on the lake let up a mournful wail. To my surprise, other loons started coming in from all directions — all landing with a great splash, already hooting and yodelling.

The loons arrived in pairs, perhaps coming from all of the surrounding lakes. They floated about in a small flotilla in front of our island, moving towards us and then away, seemingly uncertain of their direction. It was like a town council meeting, this gathering of loons. They stayed in the group, talking amongst themselves and drifting to and fro.

I've seen this on a few occasions in my life. The first time was as a youngster during a canoe trip in Algonquin Park. Forty loons or more gathered on the lake where we had set our camp. I remember my older brother was out fishing when the loons started arriving. He wound in his line and sat still, one person amongst all these birds. He drifted silently amongst the loons in his cedar strip canoe. So subtle and gentle were his paddling movements that the loons paid little attention. Then he cupped his big hands and blew into them, mimicking well the loon's crazy cry, wagging his fingers to get that staccato rhythm. Rather than being spooked, the loons seemed to answer back, arguing their point. After an hour or so, the loons started leaving, winging off in the directions they had come. The meeting was adjourned.

I saw this unique gathering of loons again some twenty-five years later, on a turquoise glacial lake in British Columbia's rugged interior. We had flown in from different directions for a tourism board meeting at a resort on Chilko Lake. A hundred loons also gathered together on the same lake in the late afternoon, discussed regional business, and then headed home.

And now, here they are gathering on our lake, a smaller group of some fifteen to twenty, perhaps only a committee meeting this time. Maybe this was their own type of G8 Summit. Possibly they are meeting to discuss the problems that we humans bring to the lake, and to work out ways

*Children bring
so much energy
to cottage life.*

to combat them. Perhaps, in these bird's eyes, the cottagers that assemble each summer at the lakes is the true "gathering of loons."

No matter the reason for the assemblage of these Common Loons, once again, it is a spectacular sight, with so many of these beautiful birds brought together. While their calls are usually hauntingly solo, here they hoot and yodel in a veritable symphony of voices.

I can't help but laugh at those that think it is time that the loon be replaced as the symbol of our wild lake country. "The Moose is the New Loon" is the rallying cry from cottage magazines and cottage marketers. Well, with all due respect to the moose, majestic, powerful, and very Canadian though it may be, the loon is still and always will be the symbol of our northern hinterland. I remember sitting by the campfire bewitched, light from the flames dancing across the white rock, when the silence of the night is pierced by the loon's cry, the wail of the insane. It is a call that is difficult to describe and impossible to forget. The guttural bawling moan of a moose is just not the same.

No one has heard the Common Loon — the mournful wails and crazy laughter that can haunt a still, dark summer's night — who will not be eternally affected by it or not associate it with the cottage on the lake. The loon has become the authentic representation of wilderness, and a vital component of it. As Henry David Thoreau said in *The Maine Woods*, "It is a very wild sound, quite in keeping with the place."

The Sting

It was the first night of our summer vacation, our first night with the family at the cottage this year. My wife and I had settled into our boathouse bunkie. I'm afraid our boathouse is a modest one, not like some of the massive buildings you can admire on Millionaire's Row. Ours is practical, small and rustic, but charming and quaint. It has a big picture window that allows a magnificent view of the lake, and we like to swing the two wooden doors open wide so we can see the stars, watch the lights shimmering on the water, and hear and smell the outdoors. A big, framed, flowing mosquito net drapes down from the ceiling over our bed, making us feel like explorers on an African safari. It protects us from pesky bugs, but does not separate us from the night.

I arrive with an oil lamp after tucking the kids away in the main cottage, to find my wife in bed under the comforter reading. "I see there's a big wasp nest under the front peak," she says nodding towards the roof front over the swinging doors.

"Really? Is it active?" I ask, and go to have a peak.

"I'm sure it is," she says, "but we can look after it tomorrow in daylight. I think I have some of that foam wasp stuff in the cabin."

By my thinking, with the wasps also tucked neatly in for the night, right now might be the time for a quick attack — and who needs the Raid. I look around and grab a paddle. My plan is simple: with one quick swing I'll bat the nest and its contents out into the lake and then I'll swing the doors shut quickly to neutralize any counterattack. My wife, seeing me walk forward with paddle cocked, begins to protest, but too late.

It almost works …

To be fair, it would have worked perfectly, if not for the sudden gust of wind. I batted the plump, pear-shaped nest just as a gust of wind blew the boathouse door shut. Like an exciting Wimbledon tennis match, the door expertly returned my serve. I did manage, most impressively I thought, considering I was using a canoe paddle, to make a nice backhand return volley. The nest hit the door once again, a second blow that, perhaps, only served to further anger the wasps. They spilled out and focussed their venom on me.

I did hear my wife laughing hysterically as I windmilled my arms and danced around the bunkie under attack. Amazingly, I was stung only once before I gracefully dived beneath the bug netting and onto the bed. The cloud of annoyed wasps buzzed the mesh. I'm not sure what you're thinking, but I'm considering myself a bit of a hero for ridding the boathouse of the venomous scourge. I half expect a big hug, to be smothered in kisses and a heartfelt "Thank you!"

Instead, I get: "It's moments like this that make me wonder what possessed me to marry such an idiot." I begin to answer but she cuts me off. "That was a rhetorical question!"

In the quiet time that follows, I'm left to muse about wasp nests and misadventures.

My father-in-law is a strong, burly man who used to be a navy diver. As such, he survived shark attacks, but a bite from a little tiny wasp could kill him. He suffered multiple stings while rescuing his son from a wasp attack, and has since become allergic. He drank one down once, presumably in a tot of rum, and had a severe reaction to a sting in his throat. My mother-in law hangs brown paper bags around whenever she is at the cottage. Her theory is that wasps and bees, being territorial, figure the bags are another's nest and stay away. Pointing out that the bags are covered with wasps does not change her opinion. Perhaps, it is her way of knocking off her husband.

"Oh, I tried everything to keep the wasps away," wink, wink, nudge, nudge. "And still, in the end, they got him."

Last summer, my oldest daughter tripped over a nest when she was playing some game of manhunt on the island. She was stung a dozen times. We heard her holler and then she darted out of the forest with a cloud of wasps in pursuit, like in some cartoon. We all dropped what we were doing and ran for the cabin — almost forgetting to let her in. If I'd had my paddle I could have staved off the attack. Not that such heroics would have done me any good.

Who Has Seen the Wind?

Who has seen the wind?
Neither I nor you:
But when the leaves hang trembling,
The wind is passing through.
        — Christina Rossetti, "Who Has Seen the Wind?"

Nothing in nature is ever exact, but it is not at all unusual for the wind on our lake to rise about ten each morning, and then die out in the late afternoon. Today it is different. It has remained still through the first half of the day, allowing the kids to get out water-skiing on a lake as calm as glass. In mid-afternoon the wind stirs up and begins to blow, whipping the water into a frenzy.

I run down to the dock to turn the boat around, so that the bow is facing out into the lake and into the wind. I tie it on the leeside so that it won't get knocked against the dock stringers, but is held away. The flags flap noisily on their pole. The wind creaks the dock, flutters the leaves, and whistles across the water and through the boathouse. It bends the tall pines, shakes the boughs, and slaps the water violently against the shore.

We secure everything that might topple off the island, except ourselves, and then settle on the dock to enjoy the blow. Any flies or mosquitoes that might have been bugging us earlier have been blown north, tumbling head over legs off to the mainland. Seagulls, who don't frequent our island, seem to love a blustery day. They circle above, screeching and soaring high on the air currents before diving like fighter jets. Two ravens sit on a branch overhead watching the antics of the gulls. They huddle together, shifting the grip of their feet while letting the wind rustle their head feathers.

Sailors have always loved and depended on the wind. On a day like today we might see a Hobie Cat, sailboarder, or small sailboat hiked out and cutting through the surf. The local bush pilot likes the waves that the wind brings, giving texture to his runway, making it easier to land.

When we were young canoeists, we used to hate the strong headwinds that seemed to always greet us on the last day of our trips, testing our mettle as we pulled hard for home. I remember one trip when my brother and I decided to wait out the wind and rollers that assailed us on our last day, on the seven-kilometre paddle up the main lake to the cottage. We pulled off to shore and fished and slept and read until darkness fell, until the wind finally deadened and gave the lake a few hours' peace.

We left at dark, paddling up the calm waters under a brilliant canopy of stars. We passed Gull Island, where the seagulls, startled awake, circled the rocky knoll, their white bodies caught in the moonlight, cackling at us for our intrusion. We pulled up to the dock at midnight and watched the mist rising from the water, the last heat in the surface being pushed into the air and swirling there in macabre patterns. We had only meant to escape the wind, but ended up having a beautiful and memorable paddle.

Our kids are not so wimpy on this day. They grab their kayaks to play in the turbulent water, jumping their bows over the foamy whitecaps. They whoop and holler, and laugh when one of their siblings gets caught sideways to a huge roller and turtles into the cool water.

Life at the lakeside cottage is controlled by the wind and the waves it brings. Our island is small enough that we can never really escape the water, never forget that it is an island separated from the mainland. Also, being an island, there is always a calm side to escape to if we wish. If the wind and waves buffet the dock, we take our chairs to swim rock on the island's north side. If the waves are breaking over our rocky swim area, we settle into our Muskoka chairs on the south-side dock.

The wind blows on into the night. The water splashes and gurgles under our boathouse bunkie's floorboards, and laps onto the rocky shore. We settle into bed listening to the water and the wind, and, in no time, its sweet lullaby has us fast asleep.

Pirates of Muskoka

I had not realized that pirates still sailed the waters of cottage country. Actually, I did not know that they ever had. Yet, here I am with my family out on Lake Muskoka, surrounded by the savage villains. Boats of every description circle our ship. The Jolly Roger flies from their sterns and their lanyards. The ugliest collection of vermin ever to sail on Muskoka's waters wave their cutlasses and swords in our direction.

Our fearless leader, Captain Hook, bellows directions to us and waves his misshaped hand around in the air. Little Johnny keeps watch with his spyglass from high above the wheelhouse and warns us of impending danger. A cannon fires from behind some cottage ramparts on Crawford Island. We swing broadside and respond in turn, giving them a taste of our own powder. Our cannonballs must find their mark, for the pirates on the shore tumble off their rocky knoll into the water.

As we pass Beechgrove Island, I can't help but notice a few lovely maidens being forced to walk the plank off a cottage dock, and I contemplate going to their rescue. I daze out for a minute and imagine myself doing a perfect swan dive off the port side, with my weapon clenched in my teeth. A few strong strokes and I'm at the dockside, fighting off the evil scallywags. There are many of them, but I am an expert swordsman. My quick rapier protects me from their blows, and soon I'm on the offensive, slashing and stabbing until all the scurvy foes are vanquished. The trio of wenches scream in delight and jump into my arms.

Water bombs burst on our ship's deck, bringing me back to the moment. I see my wife glaring at me with her hands on her hips — she knows how my mind works. "What?" I ask her, hands out in a plea of innocence.

Then the enemy is aboard, scaling the sides of the *Wenonah II*, scrambling onto the upper decks. I slink back behind my spouse, letting our brave young crew step forward in combat. They quickly send the invaders falling overboard into the icy lake waters. A raucous cheer is raised, and then we head into the galley for pancakes.

My son's soccer team had been invited out on the *Wenonah II* for a pirate cruise. I had, at first, tried all kinds of excuses for not attending, but my wife would have none of it. She loves a good theme party and also loves every chance she gets to try to make me look like a fool. She cheerily wakes me up early on this Sunday morning, having cut up my best pair of khaki pants and shredded my favourite black T-shirt, insisting that I dress the part of Long John Silver or Captain Jack Sparrow. She ties a black bandana around my head and clips a circular ring on my ear. I put on a pair of sunglasses and she shakes her head. I insist on a dusty bottle of rum in my satchel: a prop, you understand.

Of course, as soon as I'm decked out in pirate garb I immediately break into song — "Sixteen men on the dead man's chest; Yo-ho-ho and a bottle of rum!" My children roll their eyes. They are all decked out like a bunch of urchins themselves, as my wife attempts to get them into the spirit of our upcoming voyage. Well, in truth, my oldest daughter dresses the same way she outfits herself year-round to go to school.

My wife gives me a plastic, dollar-store cutlass to fight off invaders. I slice it through the air in my best Errol Flynn impression and then give her a thwack on the rump. She whacks me on the shoulder with her weapon, and I realize her giant sword is made of wood. "Drink and the Devil had done for the rest — Yo-ho-ho and a bottle of rum!"

In spite of my trepidation, it is a fun time out on the lake. With its motley group of pirates aboard, the *Wenonah II* leaves the wharf in Gravenhurst. There is a flotilla of more than twenty small boats that follow the big ship around on this day, most with young pirates aboard.

Along the mainland and on the islands we pass, cottagers dressed in full pirate attire put on their own little drama. There are soldiers and pirates; beautiful maidens, wenches, and mermaids; dandies and old sea dogs; public executions and dunkings; sword fights and treasure — everything one would expect in the romantic world of the buccaneer. Of course, it is only the *Wenonah II* crew that boards the big ship, but it delights the kids. So if you are looking for a fun way to entertain the youngsters during their cottage days, may I suggest heading out on the dangerous, pirate-infested waters of Muskoka.

Are You Afraid of the Dark?

I have to be careful what I say here, because I know that my mother reads this column, and one never wants to incur the wrath of a mother. Nor would I want her to worry that some of the psychological problems that I now have can be traced back to things she might have done. Yes, she has always had a wonderful way with kids. She can entertain them, play with them, tease them, and, if she really wants to, frighten them half to death.

I remember it vividly, as if it happened last night. We were driving down a deserted country road late in the evening (where we were going has been lost over time). My siblings and I were sitting in the back seat, undoubtedly bored, and likely asking "How much farther?" It was a dark night, with only a slight glow of moonlight. The windows were rolled down, so the warm breeze tussled our hair. Huge trees bordered both sides of the road and stretched their gnarly branches over us like a canopy. The wind blew the leaves, so it looked like giant hands were reaching for us inside the car. Our tires crunched over gravel, and the occasional screech of a bird added to the sinister atmosphere.

Presumably wanting to keep us entertained, my mother decided that this was a good time to introduce us to the "ghost song." In a spooky voice she began singing about three women in a graveyard who meet up with three ghosts. The frightful lyrics slowly build, each verse separated by a ghostly chorus, until the song ends abruptly with a climatic scream. We cowered, sinking low into our bench seat, wide-eyed and trembling. Well, it had that effect on my sister anyway; the boys were much braver, of course.

That old song might have both scared and scarred me for life, but I remember all the words and sing it now to my kids, on a dark stormy night, around the evening campfire. Whenever someone new comes to visit us at the cottage, the kids say, "We have to sing them the ghost song!"

I am not sure why we like to be scared. Why do we find delight in watching a good horror movie, reading terrifying books, or hearing macabre stories around the campfire? Ghost stories have been with us for as long as people have been telling each other stories. We love to be frightened, as long as it is not too far outside our comfort zone.

When I am travelling to some distant country, I always like taking a haunted walk. Don't get me wrong, I don't believe in ghosts, but the outings are great for giving a visitor a feel for a different culture and the history of an ancient city. If they are well done, they are fun and creepy.

I have wandered about in a massive Chinese cemetery in the middle of Kuala Lumpur, Malaysia, met historic characters amongst the dark alleys and old stone buildings of Old Montreal's historic port, taken a ghostly walk along Victoria's waterfront during the "Ghosts of Victoria Festival," and followed a black-cloaked, lantern-carrying guide through the foggy, cobblestone streets of Old Edinburgh in Scotland. All such locations were brimming with ghostly atmosphere.

There is also something about the cottage. Perhaps it is because the nights there are dark and quiet. There is the absence of the lights from town or city. The sounds are perhaps not as familiar as the ones we hear daily at home. The wind whips the branches of trees, the waves break on shore, a beaver slaps his tail, a raven gurgles, and a loon wails. Visitors to the cottage are especially susceptible to the unfamiliar.

The children insist that I tell a horrifying tale at the evening bonfire or read them a ghost story before bed. I read them "The Hook," "The Hitchhiker," and "The Weeping Woman." They tell me that the stories are lame. I read them "The Tell-Tale Heart" and "The Monkey's Paw." They are quiet. I stand up and douse the fire. We wander back in silence, single file along the well-worn path to the cottage. Shadows from a full moon dance across the white rock, playing tricks with our eyes. Blades of grass, moved by the wind, scratch across rocks, boulders that suddenly look like crumbling headstones. A pair of bats slice by in the air. The screech of what must be a gull sounds like an old woman shrieking shrilly at us.

Of course, an aspect of the ghost story for the children is to never admit to being scared. "Oh, that wasn't very scary," they will tell me after the tale — but then, before settling in for the night, they ask me off-handedly whether the doors are locked and if I wouldn't mind closing their curtains.

Bonfire

There is something about a campfire. It is mesmerizing and comforting, and a great social focal point on a dark cottage night. If the dock is the main gathering place on a hot summer's day, so is the bonfire pit on a starry, still evening. The bonfire experience also transcends the generations. It is not something that you do just to appease your kids. Nor do the younger set drop all the fun they are having to hang out reluctantly around the fire with the adults. It is something that all look forward to at the end of the perfect cottage day.

On the eastern tip of our island a solid rock outcrop juts into the lake. We call it fire rock because it has become the ideal location to sit out on a still, dark evening around a roaring bonfire. There is a shallow indentation in the granite that serves as the perfect fire pit, and flat rocks from the lake bed are stacked to shield it from the wind. Trees grow well back, a safe distance from the fire, and there are no dangerous underground roots that can smoulder out of sight. We have some log benches set around, and some pointed green willow marshmallow sticks lean against a stack of firewood.

It is a place that seems to generate conversation. The fire itself is a focal point for reflection. Staring into the smouldering coals I have come up with the inspiration for many column themes. The kids love to roast marshmallows and snack on the gooey s'mores. Young boys in particular like to poke at the flames with a sturdy stick, and then, when their stick catches fire at the tip, they stick it in the lake and listen to the hiss. Well,

I guess its not always just the kids who enjoy this; men in general seem fascinated by fires, closet pyromaniacs.

Word games are played, tall tales are told, and many songs are sung. Everyone, young and old, joins in. Grandpa often pulls his harmonica out of his pocket and plays requests. I remember guiding horse trips when I was young and carefree, week-long pack trips through Banff, in Alberta's Rocky Mountains. It's just what a young man did for work with a journalism degree in his pocket. Each evening the group would gather around the fire pit to share stories. The cook would pull out his steel-string guitar and sing all the classic cowboy tunes, his ballads and yodelling echoing off the surrounding mountain peaks, many miles from civilization. Sometimes a guest would pull out a harmonica and play along, and I would immediately long for our cottage. (Well, I'd miss my dad, too.)

Campfire traditions have been handed down — some we are not sure how they started. "I hate white rabbits," we will say when the smoke blows our way and stings our eyes. I don't know why, it is just something that is said. Imagine when we had some friends from Switzerland visit the cottage recently. Our kids are exclaiming that they hate this particular colour of rabbit. The Swiss friends look puzzled, but remain too polite to ask why we are rabbit racists with this peculiar bunny bias. When I tell them why it is said, they state matter-of-factly, "And this works? Why not just sit upwind from the fire?"

Not just at the cottage but living in cottage country, the bonfire becomes a part of many social gatherings. We recently got together with kids and parents at a wrap-up soccer party for our youngest daughter's team, at the coach's home. The lush grass in his backyard rose to a rocky knoll, with a central hollow making the perfect fire pit. Youngsters and adults enjoyed some pizza and some games, and then we gravitated to the roaring fire. The coach entertained with a guitar, and we talked with other parents that we barely knew. Standing around the evening fire encourages this.

At New Year's we gather at another friends house for an energetic shinny match on his large outdoor rink, and then warm ourselves at midnight with a glass of champagne, while standing around the roaring bonfire that burns its own deep pit in the snow and ice. How Canadian is that?

Driftwood fires on the point, where we sing, laugh, roast marshmallows, and tell ghost stories.

The bonfire inevitably brings about the feeling of togetherness and warmth. It is a great part of cottage life, sitting around the evening fire, telling the kids a ghost story before bed. The flames dance across the white rock and reflect off the shimmering lake waters. The sudden wail of a loon pierces the night, causing even the storyteller to jump. As the flames die down to glowing coals, we look up into the brilliant canopy of twinkling light searching for falling stars. Then we douse the flames and make our way back along the trail to the cottage.

That '70s Show

My parents celebrated their fiftieth wedding anniversary this past May. Fifty years together, imagine that. They were married in 1957 when *Leave It to Beaver* was the most popular show on television and "A White Sport Coat and a Pink Carnation" topped the music charts. It had been a double wedding, shared with my mother's twin brother and his wife, so now it was a double fiftieth anniversary celebration. We had a party for them, as all good kids would do. We rented a hall and invited the extended family.

We pulled out the old photos, and my sister put together a slide show presentation. With modern, PowerPoint technology, the photos faded in and out on the screen, showing the lives of my parents from their childhood days to meeting, courting, marriage, children, and then grandchildren. A musical score accompanied the presentation. It was nostalgic, heartwarming, and, at times, comical.

The early cottage days were well represented, as our cottage time was and will always be a big part of our lives. It was the summer of 1974, and my folks were paddling around the small islands in the west arm of a beautiful, pristine lake when they happened upon a hand-drawn sign: "For Sale." The "S" was actually a painted, hissing rattlesnake. They stopped in, walked the island, toured the log cabin, and fell in love with the place. The photos Dad took that day were now part of the presentation, and began a series of images that recall our fun cottage days.

There were photos of my siblings and of me doing what my kids are doing now, hanging out with friends on the dock or cottage porch, water-skiing, swimming, and canoeing. Throughout the 1970s, our family would join our cousins on an annual week-long canoe trip. Here was shared fun, hardship, and camaraderie. I was glad my own children were watching these old photos, appreciating what we had done as a family and recognizing in our canoe trips the important family values that could be learned — those that stay with you for life. I felt that they would be impressed with how tough and adventurous their dad and grandparents were.

Apparently not.

"You used to have a mullet," my son says accusingly. I cringe at the photo that shows the shaggy hair that falls down my shoulders from underneath a flat-top leather hat.

"Nice pants, Dad," chastises my oldest daughter. "Geeky!"

"They were the style back then." I try to defend myself, although I realize I am fighting a losing battle — she is right. Here is a photo of me carrying the canoe with these bell-bottom jeans on. The pants seem inappropriately tight through the midsection, so much so that it is a wonder I ever had kids myself. Then the legs sweep out in a wide bell shape that hides my entire feet — I could have been wearing high heels for all you could tell … I wasn't!

"At least Grandpa was cool," the children point out as they see a photo of my dad carrying a big canvas pack, decked out in peg leg pants, a checkered shirt, hair slicked back, and sleek dark shades, "at one time."

A photo of Grandma in a 70s-style bikini gets exclamations of appreciation. Not so, Grandpa in his Speedo on swim rock. Now it is he who is trying to defend himself. "It was the style — better than the baggy, oversized shorts you kids swim in today." Sorry, Dad, but no.

Then there is a photo of my mom's twin, Uncle John. A nice, tranquil, mood-driven canoe trip shot — he is having an early morning coffee by the open fire as mist rises from a lake. My children begin to heckle his checkered, polyester pants, but here I shut them down and tell them not to be rude. I mean, fun is fun, but this hits a little too close to home. I think he still wears them on the golf course.

It Is a Dog's Life

Timba hates when the children are in the water. When she hears a splash, she responds immediately. It does not matter whether she is dead asleep, curled nose under tail beneath the big pine, when the kids venture onto swim rock Timba comes running. She paces back and forth, trying to coax them to dry land.

Huskies are not keen water dogs, not like retrievers or collies. They are made for the cold and snow, a time when getting wet is not a great idea. Swimming to a husky is an act of folly. When the children return to shore Timba greets them with a face wash. She attempts to reason with them. When everyone is out of the lake and towelling themselves dry, Timba returns to her pine.

Charlie is a hound, a big, sad-eyed, wrinkly-faced, drooling bloodhound. He accompanies my sister's family when they visit. Charlie is in love with Timba and her blue eyes, so he tries to impress her by howling in her face. He corners her, and with his jowls quivering inches away, he howls. "Barooo, barooo, barooo!" Timba squints her eyes and lays her ears back, not totally enamoured with this crinkly, foul-breathed Casanova. Charlie doesn't listen much. He hears "No, Charlie" a thousand times in a day. You could be saying, "It's a fine day today, Charlie" for all he cares. Still, he is cute, in a very ugly sort of way.

My dad recently got a fancy new slide scanner, and he has been going through a half-century of family photos and putting them on disks that we can view on his television. As much of that family time has been spent at the cottage, many of the pictures are of us spending time on the island, slowly growing up. Through the thirty-three years of our cottage time, dogs have always appeared in the photos.

When my parents bought the place there was Bismarck, a short-legged, long-eared basset hound who trotted around the island paths going nowhere fast. His nose was too good for us kids in a game of hide-and-seek. When we went canoeing, he would sit dolefully in the middle of the canoe with his ample chops resting on the gunnels. When we ventured to the cabin in winter, he had to hop through the drifts on short legs. My brother and I would wince as he dragged his dangling parts through the crusty March snow, and then we would wince again as we watched him thaw himself by the fire.

My uncle John and his family would join us at the cottage with Toulouse, Bismarck's brother — and then, for a reason I can only put down to a mid-life crisis, after Toulouse passed on, in came Shawnee Marie, a prim and lanky Afghan. Uncle John would stand on the dock with a morning coffee, his hair messed, unshaven, dishevelled, with this groomed princess sitting prissily at his feet.

Two more bassets, Spencer (my parents') and Fred (my sister's), visited the cottage for a while. They hated each other, and would roll around in a fur flying fit of fury whenever they met. When Fred came in the front door of the cabin, Spencer was shuffled out the back.

Duke was a springer spaniel who was half loon. He would dive for rocks that were four feet deep on the lake bottom, and then build little rock cairns around the island. You could toss a rock into the boulder-strewn shallows in the bay, and he would dive in, stick his head under the water, and return with the same stone. Then there was Matty, a sweet and pretty Australian shepherd–border collie cross. My sister had gotten it right with this one. Matty would stay to the outside of the circle of children, shepherding them, whether they were playing in the forest or swimming in the lake. She would paddle around the bay for hours, always protecting, always smiling.

When I wrote the column about the death of a family dog earlier this summer, I got more feedback than for any other story, all with anecdotes of the readers' own beloved canines. One family had a wooden cross in the ground at their summer retreat, on which they hung the collars of the

For many, dogs are a big part of their cottage days, adding to the wonderful spirit of the place.

dogs that had graced their cottage lives. When they sold their cottage and bought a new one, the cross moved with them.

For many families, dogs are big part of their cottage days, adding to the wonderful spirit of the place. The only mistake in their makeup is that their lifespan is much too short. Any other shortcomings they may have are of our own doing.

Cottage Renovations

Cottage renovations are a tricky business, dependant upon such things as the remoteness of the location, access, and the ability to bring in contractors. Scheduling an electrician or plumber might delay a project for a couple of summers. Trying to get the fabulous interior design specialists John and Jon in for a consultation is impossible during blackfly season. Ultimately, having the skills of a handyman can be an essential part of being a cottage owner. Unfortunately, these skills have avoided me, but I do have talented family and friends, and I am not averse to inviting them to the cottage for a weekend's relaxation.

Our log cabin cottage was built in 1924 by a logger, purportedly for his young mistress. Two things came out of this history. Firstly, the log construction of the cottage is beautiful, with huge hand-hewn timber harvested locally. Secondly, though the logger's mistress must have had certain attributes that pleased him enough to build this humble but magnificent cabin on a remote rocky island for her, lofty stature was not one of them. The kitchen counters and sink were seemingly constructed for someone who might have helped send Dorothy off down the yellow brick road.

For a time I was able to use the cabinetry's short dimensions to advantage. When my wife would ask for my help with the evening dishes, I would pitch in for a few brief seconds and then wince in agony, grit my teeth, and grimace in extreme pain, grabbing for my lower back. My darling spouse would help me to the front porch chair, all the while apologizing for being so thoughtless, for she knew I suffered from chronic back pain. She would make sure I was comfortable, offer me an after-dinner medicinal aperitif, and then return to her solitary chore.

I believe I'm being smart in my shirking. In retrospect, I think my wife had a plan all along, a blueprint to get me to agree to a kitchen re-do, to make this part of the cottage more functional and to update the circa 1960 kitchen accents and decor. Things were working perfectly, until, on one such evening, I carried the "bad back" charade too far and unwittingly made the comment, "If only the kitchen counter and sinks were constructed at a proper height."

Immediately, as if she had long been patiently waiting for such an error in judgment, my wife dropped a heap of kitchen renovation literature into my lap: "Martha Stewart's Cottage Kitchens," "Kitchens and Bathrooms," "Kitchen and Outhouse Designs," and "Dr. Phil Reveals — How to Get Your Husband to Share in More of the Household Duties." I had opened my big mouth, and now I was trapped.

And so began the cottage kitchen renovation. My brother-in-law and sister joined us in the venture. He had a leather pouch around his waist from which dangled all his tools. I filled my jean pockets with nails, only to scream in agony when I bent over. I actually enjoyed the demolition, attacking the old cabinets and framework with a pry bar, jumping quickly on any long-lost coins that appeared, and reminiscing over any memorabilia that turned up from our youthful cottage days.

After we had torn everything apart, it came time to rebuild. We first laid down a rich red slate tile floor. With my chainsaw and drawknife, I was put in charge of the kitchen framework, which we had decided would be done in cedar log. The ladies worked outside in the sunshine fiercely whacking away at a solid pine countertop with a chain — "distressing" the wood for an antique look — something they had apparently learned from the John and Jon show. When I commented that they should be good at distressing things, I was forced to dart around the cabin, running for my life just ahead of two chain-wielding maniacs. My brother-in-law laughed at my predicament. He was in charge of the finicky finishing work.

An aged pier piling foraged from the relics of an old dam that once controlled the river inlet at the north end of the lake was hung from the cottage's kitchen ceiling with logging chains. Here, utensils, pots, and cast iron cookware hang from hooks high above the central kitchen island. It is a unique and charming piece of timber, sculpted from years of water rushing over it.

At the end of the day, we sat back pleased with what we had accomplished: a functional, charming, and rustic kitchen that fit in well with the atmosphere of the cottage.

Cottaging on a remote island can provide certain obstacles. One can not so readily hop in the car and head to town for a box of nails or the lumber for a cottage project. The marvellous sense of isolation peculiar to island cottages demands self-sufficiency and forethought.

While some cottages are really second homes, lakeside dwellings with all of the comforts, we prefer the charming rusticity of a low-maintenance escape. It is comfortable and homey, and reflects the happiness born of years of summer fun.

Our Garden Patch

Two ravens sat on a branch outside the cottage window. They sat close together while the wind rustled their head feathers and they shifted the grip of their feet. I was supposed to be working, but instead watched them with interest. These birds had always fascinated me, ever since my young days when I read Edgar Allan Poe.

The image of the raven sitting black against a bleak sky on the gnarled branch of a twisted, dead tree is ingrained in our subconscious — as much an image of horror as the thunderstorm outside the creepy, abandoned, haunted house on the hill. They mix hoarse screeches and squawks with deep-throated gurgles and garbles, while hiding in thick spruce treetops. Their human-like language is interesting in the day and spooky after dark. Their intelligence is uncanny. I have watched them steal my dog's food from his dish. One raven will hop up to the resting husky and pull on his tail. As the dog lurches unsuccessfully for the bird, another will swoop in to heist a kibble. Then they switch assignments.

These two large crows on the branch seemed to be scheming. They were staring out towards our little cottage garden patch, where my wife has tried to cultivate a few herbs, rhubarb, some lettuce, and green onions. This is no easy feat at the best of times. In fact, some would say that it is an act of folly, trying to maintain a garden anywhere in cottage country, where you are battling the Canadian Shield. She is trying to plant and maintain a garden on our three-acre mound of rock and pine, on an infertile island situated in the middle of a lake in the northern woods. The ground is nothing but a plush bed of needles and moss.

Still, she has tried. We pack over some bags of topsoil each spring and mix it with compost. We weed and plant, and weed some more. We gather stones from the lake bottom to border our patch of soil. We bring up water from the lake each day in our watering can and keep the plants wet. And the garden grows. It is great to be able to pick some lettuce for sandwiches or salads, or to harvest some herbs for the evening stew.

Then, there are the ravens. They see the garden as their own personal buffet. My wife sees all her stubborn, hard work being undermined by these birds, whom she has tried just about everything to outwit.

The other day I looked out from the cabin to the garden patch and was horrified to see myself amongst the basil and leafy vegetables, arms outstretched in a hideous manner. A floppy hat hid my face, but I could tell it was me by the manner in which I was dressed — in my good plaid shirt and my favourite ripped and torn pair of faded Levi's.

The grotesque likeness scared me, but apparently not the ravens, who flew down and perched themselves on the rigid arms. They sat calmly surveying the little garden and contemplating their lunch. At that moment my gentle wife came running up from the dock, flailing her arms and screaming like a banshee. The glossy black birds scattered in fright, winging it for the forest. Her actions panicked me as well, and I backpedalled from the window towards the safety of the cottage depths.

My wife's frightful success in scaring off the birds, where my scarecrow likeness propped amongst the vegetables had failed, caused me to later unwittingly suggest that perhaps she should spend more time standing in the garden. Oops … "If I only had a brain!"

Chirpy's Diner

I have been battling with a squirrel all day. I know what you're thinking, how could someone with my advanced intellect have any trouble outwitting a little rodent? It is a point well made, but he is a persistent little beggar.

I bought a new bird feeder for the cottage. It is called a Planet Earth Feeder, and has a spaceship design and a sloping copper roof. It also brags about holding six pounds of seed, which means I won't have to pull the ladder out as often. A weekly sanitary wipe down and a refill is all that is required. I also checked out the design with its slippery sloped metal roof, and decided that old Chirpy the squirrel would never figure this out.

It took him about one minute and twenty-two seconds.

I had hung the feeder in the fork of a long, slender branch, about twelve feet off the ground, filled it with sunflower seeds, and then I went into the cottage to brag about it to my wife. "I have finally found a squirrel-proof feeder," I said. "I've finally won over Chirpy — victory is mine!"

I led my wife to the cabin window and gave her a cocky "Ta-dah!" while pointing out the dangling feed station. She saw Chirpy sitting in it chewing on seeds, smiling, his bushy tail held erect like a victory pennant.

I ran out, throwing sticks and pine cones in his general direction. He chirped merrily away. I moved the feeder out farther on the slender branch, as far as I dared with its six pounds of seed. The squirrel ran out a side stringer and stretched his slender body across to the perch, using his tiny front feet to pull himself aboard.

I pruned back the side branches. Chirpy ran out on an upper branch, using his weight to drop it down like a drawbridge, landing him gracefully on the seed. I trimmed the upper branch. Chirpy pulled on some spandex leotards (or should have) and did his best Cirque du Soleil impression. He swung off a higher branch like a trapeze artist, before tucking his body and acrobatically performing a double revolving somersault, landing lightly amongst the birdseed.

At this point, I ran out screaming like a banshee. He went into the higher branches and chittered excitedly. My family laughed along. I brought out the chainsaw, but was warned off by my spouse.

"Just a little trimming, I could sculpt it like a Japanese bonsai tree." That would leave the beautiful mountain ash with just one spindly branch to hold the feeder.

At the sight of the saw, Chirpy ran out with full cheeks into the nearby forest. I followed; I had an idea. I took a small bag of birdseed and set it out for him under a sweeping pine. That ought to keep him happy for a while,

I thought. I came back to the cottage porch announcing haughtily that the problem was solved. No sooner had I gotten the words out of my mouth than the kids giggled and pointed to Chirpy, up in the feeder.

I threw a stick of firewood, striking the feeder and sending it crashing earthward. The glass globe shattered, the copper metal roof was bent and mangled, and the squirrel sat in the midst of the destruction stuffing seeds into the pockets of his woolly coat before prancing away into the forest.

I picked up the feeder and walked slowly, purposely into the shed, knowing that all the while my family's smiles were following me. I straightened the copper roof, gently removed all shards of glass, and then filled the lower feed bowl with seed. I grabbed a brush and some black paint and wrote on the feeder with a flourish. Then I returned it to the tree.

"Open, Chirpy's Diner."

Hunting for Hidden Treasure

It is *Indiana Jones* without the danger, *The Da Vinci Code* without the Vatican, or *Treasure Island* without Long John Silver. It is a touch of mystery, some problem solving, and some adventure. Mostly, its just a test of the imagination and something that can be done at the cottage, but not at home.

At our cottage it's lately become a tradition, not yet passed through the generations, but perhaps that will come. I am not sure why, or even exactly when it started. Like most cottage traditions it has simply evolved. For six or seven years now, when the cousins are all gathered at the cottage together, we set aside a summer's day for what the youngsters fondly call the "Treasure Hunt."

Clues lead on to clues, riddles are solved, word scrambles untangled, and anagrams deciphered. At the end of the day, the children have solved all the puzzles and find a cryptic map that leads to buried treasure. Like movie sequels, we try to make each year a little better, different, and certainly more outrageous than the previous.

The treasure itself usually is a wooden chest that contains things like little toys, water games, a new ski rope, and treats, though the booty at the end has become not nearly as important to the kids as the hunt. Even the younger children will say that the journey is more fun than the final destination, and they are sad when it is over. They say, "Dad, can you make the clues harder next time?"

I spend the better part of a day writing out clues in the form of quatrains or rhyming couplets. To find a clue pinned under the dock, a riddle might state: "Out over the water with a crib for my bed, look underneath and a clue can be read." And there the children find a new puzzle: "Never in one place but usually following you around, grab leather to hold me, a clue

Answering the call of the dinner gong.

here is found." The children chase a confused dog around to find a clue taped to its collar. You get the idea — bad poetry, but lots of fun.

In the morning, with the children still sleeping, the adults hide all the clues. In the afternoon, with our work done, we relax and watch the children wander from the forest to the cabin, from the swim rock to the dock, from the boathouse to the outhouse.

The seven cousins range in age from six to seventeen, so we allow different level clues for each. The ones designated for the youngest are a little simpler. The oldest is hit with clues that would challenge Indiana Jones. Off the kids go in a single line, meandering around the island from clue to clue. They solve the riddles, codes, and puzzles, each solution moving them closer to the ultimate prize.

Though the hunt started out strictly as a dry land exercise, it has now evolved into an anything goes affair. Often the children must don their masks and snorkels to scour the lake bottom. Bricks with letters on them are brought to the surface, then organized into words that lead the group onward. A riddle directs them to the canoes for a paddle to nearby Sawdust Island. Another clue gets them swimming out to the anchored raft, where a map is found in a bottle floating past. The pirate map has them counting paces from forked trees or rock piles, following the shadow from an old pine at sixteen hundred hours to the place where X marks the spot.

If there is any negative aspect of the hunt, it comes in the mental anguish I suffer as a result of the fifty or more clues I am forced to pen. The poetry tends to infest my brain — so I go around for days after, talking in rhymes. Like the best Shakespearean dandy, I approach my wife with a romantic ditty: "Hello, my good wife, can you please be a dear; Go up to the cottage and fetch me a beer." Her retort is a little less lyrical, and certainly does not rhyme one bit, but it does serve to break the "Treasure Hunt" spell.

In a Fog

The fog itself was not really a problem. It became an issue only because it rolled in, thick and impenetrable, on the night of the lake's annual progressive dinner. A progressive dinner is a multi-course affair, one that you begin with appetizers and cocktails at one cottage before you motor on to the next cottage for salads. Still on schedule, you depart en masse to a third cottage for the main course, with wine. With the schedule becoming increasingly harder to maintain, and the talking becoming progressively louder, it is off to a fourth cottage for dessert, special coffees, and after-dinner aperitifs.

You get the idea: a designated boat driver is a necessity. This had been factored in; the fog had not. Nor had the bevy of inebriated back-seat boat drivers who knew the lake like the back of their collective hands.

The evening began at the stroke of five, with cocktails and hors d'oeuvres at the Stewarts'. Everyone was polite and in high fashion, as Bert swung through with a drink tray and Martha explained each one of her delectable creations. At six o'clock exactly, the loquacious group leader, Idele Chatter, clapped her hands and urged everyone to finish up, it was time to be off to the Rommanes' for salad. The first tentacles of mist came creeping in from the north arm.

At 7:00 p.m. sharp, the boats meandered down to the east end of the lake, where the Sanderses had prepared Chicken Cordon Bleu. The fog had blotted out all traces of the north shore, and, when the group set off merrily at 8:30 for Crocker's Island and dessert, there was general joking and laughing about the limited visibility. Norm and Betty met the group at the dock with a lantern, even though darkness would not descend on the lake for another hour.

By 10:00 it was dark, and the fog was as thick as the proverbial pea soup. It was hard to see your own running lights. The boats left in a haphazard fashion, heading for the final destination, the party at the Cookes'. Joan Cooke had borrowed a number of records from the several ports of call, and had the LPs stacked on her knees as she headed out around Crane Island in the Crockers' boat. Betty was navigating for Norm, who could barely see the glow of the burning tobacco in his own pipe. "This way, more to the left, hold the course, veer right … hurry up, Norm, or we will miss the dancing."

Old Norm ran his powerful runabout right up onto the middle of Sawdust Island, took his pipe out of his mouth, tapped it over the side, and said not a word. The stack of records flew in all directions, fluttering down into the lake. Betty landed on her rump in the back of the boat, her stockinged legs sticking straight in the air.

I want to learn how to fly.

Betty and Joan screamed for help, but nobody seemed to hear. Some had found their way to the party, others zigzagged around the lake, lost in the fog. Joan recalled hearing the Chatters' boat idling past this way and that. Mitch was lying on the back seat with a bottle clasped lovingly in his hands, singing "Row, row, row your boat," something that was heard, along with Idele's wagging tongue, coming and going.

Her tale finished, Ms. Cooke set down her teacup. I helped her up out of her Muskoka chair on the dock and into the boat for the journey back to her mainland cabin.

My kids had found some old long-playing records while snorkelling around little Sawdust Island, an uninhabited spit of rock off our island's west point. They had no clue what they were. Some of the vinyl was in bits. Those still intact were worn thin like paper Frisbees, their jackets long since disintegrated in the water. I knew what they were, but not how they got there. I did know who to ask. Joan Cooke was one of those wise old-timers on the lake who make it their business to know everything.

"I remember the fog," Joan said as she left. "Remember that night well, 1957 … wonder we weren't all killed. Lake folk were a lot more fun in those days."

Nature's Stage

"All the world's a stage," and here, in cottage country, we are blessed to share that stage with nature.

It was rather a strange sight. My wife and I were driving near our home a few years back when we caught sight of two coyotes circling in a roadside meadow. Their heads were low, backs arched, and tails straight out like flags. There was something in the field they were stalking. We pulled over to watch. Suddenly, as the coyotes closed in, their quarry spread its wings wide in a ferocious display of size. We recognized the hunted as a red-tailed hawk, injured and grounded. The canines had the intention of making this predator their prey.

Now, I'm usually one to let nature run its own course, but my wife felt badly about this mismatch and ordered me to go to the bird's aid. I grabbed my camera as an assault weapon and into the breach I ran, hollering like a lunatic. The terrified coyotes ran for cover. The red-tailed hawk, rather than being thankful, found a new target for his anxiety. He fluttered his massive wings and bounced towards me. To show that my intentions were more honourable than those of the previous antagonists, I knelt down and spoke quietly to the frightened bird. While my wife drove quickly home to get a blanket and to make a couple of phone calls, I took some wonderful photos. I had never been so close to such a magnificent hawk. The red-tail gradually calmed, his outstretched wings slowly closed.

Knowing that if we left the hawk there it would not survive, we carefully captured him in a heavy blanket and drove to a nearby veterinarian for advice. We were told that the hawk had damaged wing feathers that would heal in time. If we could keep him safe for about a month, the hawk should fully recover. We took the red-tail home and housed him in a spare chain-link dog kennel, six by ten feet, and eight feet high. The enclosure was open at the top, so when the hawk was well enough, he had the freedom to leave. We caught mice in a trap to feed our patient. The bird would never eat while we watched, but he must have been thankful, because the mice always disappeared.

After two weeks the hawk got braver and more mobile. He would screech at us when hungry, and moved off his perch and around the enclosure. After just three weeks of rehab, the beautiful bird disappeared. Healthy again, the red-tailed hawk took to the skies.

I must admit, we were quite pleased with ourselves. We had stepped in to help this beautiful bird, and were successful in our cause. I wondered whether, in some heartwarming Disney-esque way, the red-tailed hawk had formed a special bond with us, his protectors. Maybe, someday, when I was in trouble, our friend the hawk would fly in to save me.

Apparently not.... As I worked outside the next day I heard a terrified cacophony of clucking and confusion coming from our chicken coop. (Yes, we used to raise a few chickens.) I ran to the rescue, just in time to see our hawk flying off with a young chicken clutched lovingly in his talons. Who could blame the bird? As the hawk had pecked fussily at our trap-killed mice, across the way he had watched, day after day, our nice, plump chickens strutting about in their coop. He must have thought us very poor hosts indeed.

In most places it is solely a human drama that plays out in people's lives, on the streets around them and on the nightly news. As cottagers and those living in cottage country, we are blessed with a region where we often see moose, black bears, foxes, deer, groundhogs, rabbits, beavers, loons, herons, ducks, and various other splendid creatures. These birds and animals are the players who take a leading role on our stage, and the production is grand.

Autumn Colours

Back to School

Summer is over. Well, not officially, but the children are back to school. When I was a youngster, summers seemed to last forever. Now they disappear in the blink of an eye. It's not just me, either — everyone I talk to complains that they do not know where the summer has gone.

The kids are excited about seeing their friends, even though the desire to be back in the classroom is not something that they would openly admit to. I am a little sad. I know that having the children board the school bus every morning will leave me with more quiet time to work. I also know that the lake is beautiful in autumn, and we will escape to the cottage at every weekend opportunity. Still, those fun family times at the cottage this year are drawing to a close. It seems like only yesterday that we were opening up the place.

Perhaps summers seem to go by more quickly because we are busier now. We juggle our cottage time with soccer schedules, hockey camps, dance competitions, family obligations, and, well, work. We fill up our calendar. Then we fill up our cottage days with a list of projects that we need to get done. In the end it becomes a race against the clock, and we watch the end of summer closing in on us with shocking speed.

As youngsters, we would wake up mid-morning in the boathouse bunkie, grab a little breakfast, and then look at each other and say, "So, what should we do today?" We had no schedule, no to-do list, no day-timer with pages filled. We enjoyed each day to its fullest, and approached each day with no expectations. The days seemed long, and I can only imagine how long they would have seemed if we had gotten out of bed at a decent hour.

Our children are the same. They run around the forest for an hour playing some adventure game. They huddle and ask the question, "What

To return to those endless summers of our youth, perhaps we need only to act like children again.

do you want to do now?" They go for a swim, go water-skiing or canoeing. They find enough level ground for a baseball match. They participate in some form of Cottage Olympics. Their days are filled with activity from the time they crawl out of bed in the morning until the late hour when they play a board game at the kitchen table or tell a ghost story at the bonfire.

A theory begins to form in my mind. To get back to those seemingly endless summers we enjoyed as youngsters, perhaps we need only act like children again! To test this thesis, I decide to join in on the Cottage Olympics. My children, their cousins, and their friends are participating in a triathlon today, running the trail that follows the shoreline, swimming out to and back from the swim raft, and finally kayaking around the island. The children are all a-twitter at the prospect of their dad simply surviving, but I am an athlete from way back. The early run goes well, and I imagine myself breaking all cottage records. Then my legs start getting a little heavy, and I stumble over the last few rocks and roots.

I peel off my runners and dive into the lake, doing what I fancy is a beautiful front crawl — that is, until my weighty legs begin to sink. The front crawl becomes a breast stroke, then a side stroke, and then, as it gets close to becoming just a stroke, I manage the last few metres with a dog paddle. The children steady the kayak for the last leg of the race, and, as I jump nimbly into the craft, I perform half of an Eskimo roll that I simply assumed was part of the event. I empty the kayak and then start the paddle around the island. I will later contend that the wind picked up against me, and this is why my time is slightly behind my six-year-old's.

For the next two days I struggle around the cottage with aching lungs, sore limbs, and tender muscles. These painful days seem longer somehow, so I know that my endless summer theory is correct. Still, when they try to convince me to join in on the decathlon, I politely decline. Unfair, I say, that an athlete of my advanced ability should be involved. Instead, I settle in with a beer and the stopwatch as official timer. Summers that seem to last forever are best left to the experts.

I'm a Lumberjack

There are a couple of activities at the cottage that always draw spectators. One is backing the boat and trailer down the boat ramp into the lake. Men appear out of the forest from nowhere to watch. As you drive slowly up to the public boat launch there seems to be nobody around. This pleases you greatly, as it makes the whole process much easier. You are an expert when unwatched, and can swing the truck around with a flourish, throw it into reverse, and back truck and trailer straight as an arrow down the narrow ramp.

So you slink up to the launch and spin the vehicle and trailer around, all the while watching for onlookers. Your wife offers to jump out to help guide you back. You acquiesce, because it is easier, though you know that she will stand in a blind spot and become yet another obstruction for your driving. If she does suddenly and frighteningly appear within the view of your truck mirrors, she will be making such contorted signals that you will really have no clue as to what she is trying to convey. Still, you let her help out from the outside, because it is better than having her try to help from the inside. Inside she will give directions and lean forward to look out of your review mirrors herself, so that when you throw a glance to the passenger side mirror, you see only the back of her lovely new hairdo.

Just as you throw the truck into reverse to begin the simple procedure, you look around and are startled by the gathering throng of men. They appear from everywhere — some have tools still in hand, some carry a fishing rod or lug along a stack of wood in their arms. Some walk in hip waders, others drive four-wheelers. The crowd comes out of the woodwork, like an old episode from *The Twilight Zone* where the mob gathers to stare at a traffic accident.

The staring assemblage has a certain effect on your ability to drive. It is like the first tee on a golf course, when you lead off with what will be your worst drive of the day, shanking the ball almost directly right before listening to the mock applause of the beer-toting spectators lounging on the clubhouse deck.

Normally you are quite adept at backing up trailers. Now, watched, you zigzag down the ramp, fishtail your trailer, jackknife, and pull forward and back, all the while watching your wife's handy gesticulations. The gathering of men greet your attempt with either a silent nod (meaning thumbs-up) or a grimace and a slow shake of the head (meaning thumbs-down). Then the crowd vanishes back into the trees. It is like they were never really there.

My brother-in-law works for the coast guard out of Vancouver. Their main facility on the Pacific sits next to a very public boat launch. When each yacht, sailboat, and motorboat arrives to be backed down the ramp, these government workers gather to hold up scorecards, like the honest judges in a figure skating competition. When a rich captain jackknifes his million-dollar yacht, he is able to stare out at scores ranging from 1 to 3, and see his tax dollars at work.

The other cottage activity sure to gather a crowd of skillful onlookers is the felling of a tree. Like the athlete competing in the big game, the pressure is on. They watch you set the notch, check the wind, judge the lean and the warp of the trunk, and then cut the hinge, all the while nodding their heads in agreement or shaking their heads in quiet disbelief. All the watchers are, of course, experts.

The best lumberjack can drop the tree on a dime. I'm not bad with a saw; I can carve up wood to build a log table for the dock or a big log frame for a bed in the A-frame tent. In backcountry camps I have sculptured a hewn log easy chair with a chainsaw and axe. I can usually drop a tree approximately where I want it. Sometimes when I have people watching, I try to hurry the process to impress the spectators. That is usually a bad idea.

Usually I'm quite accurate with my tree felling. At other times, my dad is watching. Even as we get on in years, we always want to please our dads, make them proud of what we've learned in life. Usually wanting to show him my expertise with a chainsaw only leads to him having to scramble out of the way of a tree that has inexplicably tumbled backwards, the opposite direction from what was intended, the tree only slightly missing his scurrying backside.

Such is life. We hit the hole in one while golfing solo. We score our hat trick or hit that grand slam when our parents miss one of our games. When we want so badly to please them we almost drop a heavy maple tree on their heads. They love us anyway.

Inspector Gadget

Let me be totally honest, I am not very fond of heights. That is why stepping off a mountain at four thousand metres with nothing but nylon webbing separating one from certain death would seem a strange thing for me to be doing. Still, there I was, paragliding over the Aeswritch Glacier and getting a bird's-eye view of the Alps and the neat, orderly nature of the Swiss landscape.

I suppose I deserved this. My wife and I had become friends with a Swiss couple, Alain and Nicole, who live just outside Zurich. They had joined me on a dog sled expedition some twelve years earlier. I had taken them out into Canada's wintery wilds and forced them to brave frigid temperatures that dropped into the minus-forties. I gave them their own sled and sent them careening down a mountain trail pulled by a team of excited huskies.

Next up was a summer visit when I guided them around British Columbia's Bowron Lakes canoe route. I forced these novice canoeists to tackle some whitewater, high winds, nasty whitecaps, and pelting rain on a week's canoe excursion. In the evening I threw in a grumpy grizzly, a mother moose, and some of my camp cooking, not knowing which was the most dangerous.

So now they have encouraged us to visit them, and have finally found payback. There I was, facing my fears, spinning like a kite in space, ten thousand feet above the ground. The day before, my wife and I had been to the top of the Matterhorn, in a manner of speaking. Aboard a helicopter, we drifted close enough to the summit to see the ropes that dangle down the south face and the climbers' hut, used as a resting place before adventurers set off for the summit. The helicopter had taken us climbing vertically up the rock wall, breaking over the crest before plummeting down the other side in a stomach-churning joyride, making me long for solid ground under my feet.

That was last spring. In the fall, our Swiss friends came to our cottage for the first time. They experienced a Canadian Thanksgiving there, and enjoyed the vibrant autumn colours of Muskoka. They were amazed. I had threatened them with bungee jumping, hot air ballooning, or a barrel ride over Niagara Falls. In the end, I decided to call a truce and give them the relaxing peace and quiet of cottage country.

We did get a little active. We enjoyed a dinner cruise on Lake Muskoka aboard the *Segwun*. We did some canoeing and a little hiking in Algonquin Park. The most dangerous thing we did on this visit was to jump into the chilly lake waters on an October afternoon; more dangerous for me, because Alain favours those European-style swimsuits.

Whatever adventure we set out on, our Swiss friends showed up looking like they had just been in a photo shoot for *National Geographic*. Off on our hike on a drizzly day, I had an old, tattered oilskin slicker on. It went well with my green rubber rain pants that are too short, ending somewhere just below my knee, making me look like Li'l Abner. Alain was smartly attired in a breathable Jack Wolfskin GORE-TEX jacket and pants, with matching gloves and state-of-the-art, battery-operated hiking boots.

I am not a techy kind of guy. My kids are always disgusted with me as I try to figure out how to use my cellphone. Alain, on the other hand, loves technology and has every modern gadget known to man. The watch on his wrist was right out of the world of James Bond. It checked his heart rate, chimed when he needed to hydrate, and let him know what time it would be if he were hiking in Switzerland or in China, as opposed to Muskoka.

He had a Swiss Army knife on his belt with enough tools and implements for it to fully replace everything in your cottage work shed. His BlackBerry doesn't work at our cottage, which unsettled him, but his GPS was in fine form, and allowed him to find his way to and from the privy and around the shoreline of our three-acre island. He carried it in his hand throughout the day's hike, and stared at it as much as at the beautiful scenery.

We climbed up to a rock precipice that provides a splendid view over the lake and valley. "How high up do you think we are?" asked my wife.

"Oh, I'd say somewhere between three and four hundred metres," I responded.

"Actually we are at three hundred twenty-seven," pointed out my resourceful friend, looking at the little gadget in his hand. "Perhaps we should enjoy a little rest. My watch tells me my heart rate is a little high after that climb. So does your heavy breathing," he added, smiling.

Of course I made due fun of him for his dependence on technology. I snickered and rolled my eyes, drawing the ire of my most tolerant spouse. I sat down on a jagged rock and pulled out a bottle of water and an energy bar. Alain slipped off his day pack, unlashed a metal tube from the side, and from it flipped open a number of lightweight, comfortable cushioned stools. His small pack transformed itself into an elaborate picnic basket, complete with a bottle of red wine, glasses, an assortment of fanciful cheeses, and French bread. The ladies sidled up to him.

I borrowed his Swiss Army knife — for the corkscrew, of course. After all, some gadgets are simply invaluable.

Splitting Wood

I sit on the front porch and sharpen the axe with a stone and the chainsaw with a file. Fall is the best time for bucking up logs and splitting wood. The air is fresh and cool, the ground is clean and blanketed with a crunchy carpet of colourful leaves, and there are no blackflies or mosquitoes pestering you as you work. The frustration that is born from getting nipped behind the ears by small flies that buzz around your head while you are holding an axe in your hand can be a very dangerous thing.

After some time sitting working at the laptop, I love heading out and taking out my frustrations by whacking some maple logs with my splitting maul. I take down a standing dead birch and then buck it up into twelve-inch logs that will fit in the wood-burning stove. We don't have much hardwood on the island: a little bit of maple, some birch, lots of pine, and some cedar that makes the best kindling.

I grab the splitting maul and set the logs on the chopping block. I take a quick look to find the sweet spot and to avoid the knots. Feet shoulder width apart, the lower hand at the end of the handle, the upper one starting halfway up and then sliding down easily as the arc of the axe falls. At the precise moment the axe strikes comes a flick of the wrist to halve the log like it was fastened by a spring.

My energetic wife often offers to help, but I hold up my hand. "This, my dear, is men's work — are there no dishes to be done or floors to mop?" Now, before any of you skillful female foresters go running for your keyboard to send a letter off to my editor, let me say that I'm kidding, of course. Just trying to outpoint my darling wife in the daily tennis match of barbs. Besides, there seems to be a dwindling number of tasks where a man can feel like a man. Such tasks as felling trees, splitting firewood, backing up boat and trailer, and cooking steaks on the barbecue. The truth is, after I've finished making a mess splitting, I welcome my wife's help picking up and piling the firewood.

Today, I put in a few hours filling up the woodbox and splitting wood into a huge hill that surrounds my chopping block. "You'd better get cleaned up," says my wife. "We have company coming for dinner. We can pile the rest of the wood tomorrow." I think about our invited guests and whack a few more logs.

I grab a cold beer from the fridge to wash away the sawdust, then head down to the boathouse to fill the washbasin for a quick clean-up. I wipe away the sweat and dirt and then soap and rinse my hair, grab a towel, and sneak out back to swim rock for a quick dip in the refreshing lake. I hear our guests arriving in their boat, so I towel off, put on my cleanest dirty shirt, and make a half-hearted attempt to comb my hair. I wander back up to the cottage to find our island neighbours admiring my dear wife as she stands amongst the recently split logs and hatchets a couple pieces of cedar into kindling.

"Girl," says the visiting wife, "you just never stop, do you? I smell supper on the stove, the place looks lickety clean, and here you are chopping wood to keep the place cozy and warm to boot."

"Where's your husband, anyway?" asks her husband. "Off having a nap in the hammock?"

"Oh, here's Jamie now," says my sinister spouse. The invited guests turn my way. They see me with a beer in hand, looking fresh and clean. He admires me with reverence. His wife greets me with a scowl. I can't help but notice a little smirk on my wife's face: she has gotten me back for my crack about the dishes and floor. I give her a wink, conceding the point.

I enjoy getting out on a colourful autumn afternoon to buck and split wood for the fireplace. It is especially rewarding when the smell of burning wood and the sight of wispy smoke hanging above the cottage chimney greets the senses on a cool September morning, or when we are able to relax in front of the cabin fire in the evening with a dram and a good book. We feel a certain sense of cottage comfort — warm, cozy, and satisfied.

Season's Change

As I am writing this, the sun is shining brightly in the late-afternoon sky, making me squint to view the screen of my laptop. I am sitting at the large pine table in the cottage, looking out at the lake. The autumn sun is still powerful enough for the solar panel to keep my computer batteries fully charged, and the freshness of this season inspires me. I have the barbecue on outside and have been entrusted with minding the hamburgers.

It is nearing the end of September, and I am ruminating about all the things I love in this beautiful season. We are enjoying a fantastic fall on the heels of a superb summer. Autumn is perhaps my favourite time of year, or do I only feel that way because it is here now? The spring and summer bugs — mosquitoes, deer flies, and blackflies — are long gone.

The colours are spectacular. The leaves of the maple, birch, and aspen gradually turn golden, red, or orange as the nightly temperatures drop. They fall from the trees and leave a beautiful carpet along the walking trails. It feels spongy underneath hiking boots, so footsteps make little sound. The heavy green summer foliage shrinks back and opens up new views and vistas.

The lake is no longer a pleasant temperature for a swim, but the water holds enough warmth for what we call a refreshing dip. It takes a little longer to work up the courage to take the plunge — I stand on the rock staring down at the water. I make up my mind to dive in and ready myself, and then find some excuse to put it off for a while longer. Finally, the heckling of the kids becomes unbearable, and in I go. Scrambling back out and towelling off, one feels clean, refreshed, and invigorated.

In the dawn, an eerie mist shrouds the lake, settling in the bays and rocky inlets. Smoke from the chimney hangs still in the chilly morning air. I love to rise early, to paddle around the island and feel the cool mist lick my face, when the day still smells of dawn. Sometimes we sit with our coffees on the dock and watch the mist rising from the water, swirling there in macabre patterns.

The cool, crisp autumn air seems more conducive for outside work than the hot, humid, oppressive days of summer. I love to buck and split firewood, stacking it in the lean-to shelter. We do the little things to get the cottage ready for winter. We work at renovating the cottage porch, stopping to watch the geese fly by overhead in graceful formation — a portent of approaching snow.

We are not the only ones who are busy: squirrels bustle about, gathering and storing, laying berries and seeds out on old stump-tops to dry in the autumn sun, and tossing cones down from the towering conifers. They chitter noisily at our pesky dog, who has upset their autumn routine.

The days are shorter now and the nights are cool; the starry sky seems all the more brilliant. I stay up late reading or working under the lantern

A love of the water.

light, listening to the light snaps and hisses of wood in the stove. The fire dies to coals. I pull the wool sweater over my head and crawl beneath the down quilt where my wife sleeps. There is still a slight smell of kerosene in the air from blowing out the lamp. The autumn silence is profound; only rarely do sounds permeate the night.

I am reminded that some places do not have a winter, summer, spring, or fall; just sunny days and rainy days, bright days and bleak days, warm days and hot days. As for me, I love the seasons. I love autumn all the more because of summer, and spring because we have endured a winter ... but I must go now, the late September sky has suddenly blackened, as smoke billows from the barbecue.

Three Men on a Dock

I read somewhere that men, on average, use three thousand words a day. I would imagine that most are smaller words, and many are used more than once. The report had women, comparatively, using twenty thousand words per day (or was that per hour, I can't quite recall). I have trouble envisioning how they work out these numbers. Does some scientist follow a select group of people around all day, putting a little tick on a paper each time they open their mouths? I find the number a little high, quite frankly ... for the men, I mean.

I have met some talkative sorts, a few men on steady transmit, but my experience is that a good many live by the same adage as I do: "Why use up any of your daily word quota if a simple grunt will do?" We are able to sit in a group through the full three periods of a local hockey game and not utter one syllable, other than to interrupt the chatter of our wives, from time to time, to inform them that their son or daughter has just scored. We never even come close to using up the purchased minutes of our cellphone account, even though the number of times the phone is used can be high. In fact, I'm sure if some outsider tapped into our phone conversations, it would be quite painful.

Three guys had gotten together to remove some trees that leaned dangerously over the rooftop of a riverfront cottage. Three arms of a stout maple tree listed badly over the home's Muskoka room, looking like a strong breeze would send them crashing through the roof. The owners of the quaint cottage were worried. They also happened to be away at the time.

The expert at tree-felling, aptly nicknamed Woody — undoubtedly because of his experience in forestry — was the boss and leader on this day. He went about his business with an understated precision, while uttering a few brief instructions to his two helpers from time to time.

The trees dropped where he wanted them, and we worked away in silence, limbing, bucking up the timber, stacking it, and cleaning the debris. Many times we considered quitting for the night, but no one would volunteer to be the first to stop, so we soldiered on until the task was complete. The warm summer evening had us wet with sweat, and the sawdust had us dry, so we retired to the dock to cool ourselves with a few frosty beverages.

Sitting there looking out over the peaceful water, we began to talk. We talked about toys, trucks, tools, and fancy new gizmos that made it easier to drop a tree. We remembered famous old characters around the lake, now departed. We discussed our cottage plans and the projects we would undertake someday soon, and promised to help each other out in these endeavours. We spoke about sports, of course, about hockey, both pro and our boys in the local minor league. We talked about the Olympics, just past, how amazing a swimmer named Phelps was, how fast a Jamaican called Bolt could run, and what a cool name that was for a sprinter.

At times we talked seriously, at times we tried to be witty and funny, and we shared some good laughs. We considered putting a couple of the branches and treetops of the fallen timber over the peak of the roof, spreading some glass fragments around in the driveway, and fastening some plywood over the big glass windows of the Muskoka room. The dangerous trees were at the back of the cabin, and the laneway came in from the front, so we thought this lark might bring on a funny reaction upon the owners' return. Then again, we thought we might never be forgiven, and we knew the lady of the house would get even, so we scrapped the idea.

The sky darkened, and we babbled on about the stars and how magnificent they appeared at the cottage. We mentioned how the nights were getting cooler now, and how nice it would be to build a sauna here by the lake. We discussed sauna designs and deliberated on how to best distribute the heat, described how so-and-so had ingeniously constructed theirs.

We schemed about going on a gentlemen's ski trip out west together next winter, taking our sons with us. We debated on how best to broach the subject with our wives.

We yarned on about the crazy jobs we had when we were young, the adventures and the silliness. One had been a hockey player, one a cowboy, and the third a firefighter. We realized we hadn't known a lot about one another. Now we were settled down with more mature jobs, families, and commitments. We were just three friends, three cottagers, sitting on a dock in the evening with our chores done for the day.

I think we may have used up a whole week's quota of words before we decided to call it a night and wander home. I'm sure it will even out, though, when we see each other over the next few days and offer a brief grunt as a greeting.

Autumn's Spell

I drive along one of the pretty, meandering back roads of cottage country through the warm enchantment of a sunny afternoon, passing through rock cuts of pink granite, dipping down through valley bottoms, and moving alongside leaden lakes now quiet after the summer rush. The road flings itself around the shoulders of hills, dips, and rises and carries on through a quiet forest. I drive in solitude, thinking that here, in autumn, I have this roadway all to myself.

The road crosses a bridge, climbs a small hill, and then straightens along the side of an open valley. I am surprised to see a tour bus pulled over where the shoulder widens, a group of people standing gaping off across the vale. They have their cameras out and arrange themselves in small groups taking photos, with the far hillside as a backdrop. At first I wonder what they see, and slow to look for a moose or bear. I see nothing but a valley and distant knoll.

I slowly manoeuvre around them, shake my head, and carry on, a little annoyed that this herd of tourists has invaded my quiet excursion. The road climbs a little higher and then snakes through a wide meadow. Suddenly, I see it. The late-afternoon sun throws its enriching light over the hillside. An explosion of colour: vivid reds and vibrant oranges mixed with golds, greens, burgundies, and yellows overpower the senses.

This kaleidoscopic display butts up against a rocky escarpment and sweeps down to the narrow bay of a Muskoka lake. Here the colours are mirrored in the shimmering royal blue of the water. It is like a painting. The view is awe-inspiring. I pull off to the side and grab my camera. The bus chugs past and I see smiling faces turned my way, much nicer than the slightly annoyed look I so recently gave them. I wave, a salute and a thank you for helping me to see.

Sometimes we can get a little complacent about the beauty of the world around us. We would rather find the spectacular when we go looking for it, in the far-away places we visit, but we neglect it right under our noses.

I lived in the West for quite some time, amongst the snow-capped mountain peaks of the Rockies. Sometimes I would get so used to my surroundings that I became blind to their spectacular appeal. I was working in the tourist trade, however, and was always reminded by visitors how lucky I was to be living in such a lovely setting. For a time I lived in Banff, and would walk to work in the early morning hours, stepping around wild elk that wandered through the townsite, not giving them a second look, treating them as I would late-night revellers finally making their way homeward. Sometimes the charm and wildness of our surroundings becomes so commonplace that we lose our ability to see. I imagine that this happens to people the world over. They might ask themselves, "Why are all these people here taking photos of ruins. Where is the beauty in that?"

Since I have moved back east to Muskoka, I have had scores of people ask me why I left such a spectacular part of the world to settle here. Have they not looked around themselves, at the wild hardwood forests, the inviting lakes, and the rugged beauty of the Canadian Shield?

I am on my way to the cottage. It is time to close the place for winter. I set out on my journey in kind of a sullen mood, but the big views of rock, blue-green lakes, and the resplendent colours of the forest have done their work. I know when I arrive at the lake and trek up the path to the cabin, I will enjoy the thick, vibrant carpet that cushions my steps. I will look skyward at the geese flying south. There will be the wonderful smells and textures of the fall-cured grasses and the slightly decaying odour of fallen leaves. In the evening there will be the smoky smell of the woodstove and the soft glow of the lamplight. Perhaps the cold, crisp night sky will welcome me with a magnificent display of stars, or even the northern lights. This is a beautiful place in the world, as the busload of tourists I passed well knew.

I was not looking forward to this trip to the cottage, but now autumn has cast its spell, and I am thankful.

To Fetch a Pail of Water

It was snowing when we opened the cottage on the long weekend in May. Now, while it was not exactly snowing when we came to close the place, it was far from warm summer weather. Things were so busy at home that I grabbed my dad and a couple of dogs to head up to the lake mid-week, driving through the beautiful colours of a spectacular autumn day. We looked forward to this visit. It would be a great bonding time for father and son, and we wondered when, if ever, we had been to the cottage together like this, just the two of us.

It was cold. We awoke the first morning to see our breath. A heavy mist rose from the lake, and the dock was covered by a thick, white frost. We had already dissembled the pump, so I wandered down to get a bucket of water for the breakfast dishes. My dad's footprints were clearly etched on the frozen pier boards where he had grabbed a pot of water for morning coffee. It made a beautiful photo, the swirling fog, the white frost on the dock and boat, footprints of Dad and dogs, and the distant beams of light from a sun trying to poke through to lend a little warmth to the scene.

Our cottage is a little remote, so we tend to close up the cabin like a fortress. Our main intention is to protect the place against intruders — from vandals, but more so from furry trespassers. We bolt heavy wire mesh on all of the windows. Seldom have we had much trouble with the cabin from people. The mice and squirrels have at times left a mess in the interior, as they have enjoyed the run of the place through the cold months. Over time we have learned how to close the place to minimize the damage.

We secured the cabin, packed up any foodstuff that remained from our summer visits, put anything that might freeze over winter away in our bunker below frost line, and stowed all the bedding and towels that the mice might find inviting into secure closets. We worked our way through our closing checklist, and by evening had pretty much everything done.

We had a nice steak dinner, and Dad and I talked about all the great years we had enjoyed in this place. We reminisced about the adventures and the misadventures, the lessons learned, the fun times and the growing up that we had done here. After dinner, I settled down at the table to work on this narrative; it was my last column of the season, and I was unsure what to write.

"Can't help you there," said my dad, and then disappeared outside to grab a kettle full of water for cleanup.

I worked away, writing down little notes and trying to find some inspiration. I was unaware that while I was agonizing over a storyline for some time, my dad was outside doing his best to supply it.

The two huskies had wandered down with him and watched from the end of the dock as he leaned over to scoop some water. It was dark, and the water was smooth and black; it was hard to tell where night air ended and cold lake water began. The dogs watched him tumble into the water and splash around trying to find his footing and struggle back to dry land. In the movies they would have raced up to fetch me, offered up a bark of danger, a yelp that said, "Put your pen down, stupid, the old guy is in trouble!"

When the door of the cabin swung open and he stood there dripping on the stoop, this was the point that seemed to disconcert him the most. (Well, besides the fact that he realized immediately that his exploits would be in the paper in a week.) "They just stared down at me," he complained, "I'm sure wondering what I was up to. They stood there side by side with their heads cocked to the side and an inquisitive expression on their faces. When I got out, they ran away scared, like I was the creature from the black lagoon."

That made me laugh — he looked a little like that. His sweatshirt was soaked, stretched long and dripping. His hair was in a soggy state of disarray. His shoes squelched as he walked, and he left a long trail of water behind, like swamp ooze. He shivered uncontrollably, but tried to tell me that the water was actually quite beautiful.

"I'm not going for a swim, Dad."

"No, it felt surprisingly nice, and I feel clean."

I think it is great when you feel so good when you should really feel ridiculous — but I didn't tell him, of course. After all, he is my dad. Besides, it kind of scared me. What if he had hit his head and drowned? What would I tell my mom? "Sorry, but I had to leave Dad in the lake, he was too water-logged for me to lift." Would I ever get a lecture. "See," she would probably tell me, "I knew your lack of enthusiasm for doing the dishes would someday lead to trouble."

It will be another cottage tale. It will be a story made better over time. Someday I will be closing the place with my son. How special is that? I'll grab a bucket and head out in the evening for some water. I will pause on the front porch, remembering adventures from days past — then I will slip on a life jacket and head for the dock.

The Closing

I put the metal screens on the cabin windows. They bolt on and make our log cottage secure over the winter. The pump is dismantled and drained. The propane tanks are stored and the lines sealed against insects. My wife rummages through the cupboards, packing unused food away in boxes to take back home. She fortifies the kitchen drawers and cabinets against little, furry winter intruders.

The canoes go to the boathouse, with the life jackets, paddles, water skis, tow ropes, and tubes. We turn the soil in our little garden patch. The Muskoka chairs are moved from the dock to the shed. I lower the Canadian flag on the dockside pole, fold it neatly, and store it away. Everything has its place. The closing ritual is a time-honoured affair, perfected over the years. Well, perfected, but never perfect. There are always important things forgotten and lessons learned — often little things discovered when it is time to open the cottage in the spring.

I clean the duck nesting box and change the straw bedding. We have had a female merganser roosting in the box the past two springs, and we, of course, are happy that we can help out in a small way. Even happier in

May, when I thought that the wooden house was empty and joked that I should hang a vacancy sign, but when I tried to peek in the little entry hole I was greeted with a terrifying hiss. I fell backwards from my perch, much to my family's delight. We knew then that we would enjoy watching a young merganser brood trail around behind their mother in our bay and find pleasure in seeing the youngsters mature and grow through the summer months.

While the opening of the cottage is always anticipated with excitement and done with smiles, the closing is a necessary but melancholy end to the cottage season, done with a heavy heart. If we can find the time, we may sneak up for a weekend or two in late October or November. We may even snowshoe or sled over to the island for a winter visit, but those fun family cottage days of summer are officially over for another year.

The cabin stands lonely.

This year as we close the cottage, the weather is appropriate. The wind blows the fallen leaves around and whips the lake into a frenzy. A steady drizzle falls, and everything is damp. The maple and birch trees are empty of their colourful foliage and stand stark and naked. The sky is grey and sullen. It suits our mood.

With everything loaded in the boat, my wife and I take one last stroll around the island trail. We stop to admire the tree fort that the children have built this summer, high up in some pines — too high for my comfort level. We pause at the rock cairn that marks our dog Macky's resting place. We wander out the plank walkway to swim rock and look out over the water that was so blue and inviting during the summer months. Now, though beautiful still in its own way, it is cold, choppy, and leaden grey. We pass by the point where we enjoyed many bonfires on those still summer evenings. Here, we sang some songs, were entertained by my dad's harmonica, told some tall tales, and scared ourselves with ghost stories. My wife and I stack the wooden benches neatly under the sweeping boughs of an old pine tree.

Finally, knowing that it is time and we can delay no longer, I have one last look in the cabin and lock and bolt the door. We head down to the dock. I imagine squirrels watching us from the tree branches, our friendly mink peering from his hollowed log on the shore, and the mice eyeing us from the woodpile.

All of them saying, "Good, those strange creatures are finally leaving. We can have our cottage back!"

In Winter Snow

Cottage Country Christmas

I sometimes wonder how certain traditions come to be. I am, in fact, wondering now as I hang precariously off the roof of my Muskoka home.

My upper torso is suspended in space beyond the roof eaves as I work at untangling a web of wire and lights. The toes of my winter boots are dug into the icy, shingled slope. My fingers, numb from the cold, fumble with the bulbs. Far below me I see the white ground, and I am fully aware that our mild weather lately has left very little snow to break my inevitable fall.

Below, I also see my wife staring upward, and I am touched that she is there to catch me when I fall. I realize she is pointing and shouting up instructions as if my exercise is a simple matter akin to rearranging the living room furniture. "You have two yellows together," she seems to be shouting, but her words blow off in the biting wind. My three daughters stand at my wife's side, echoing her commands and offering their own helpful suggestions.

The ladies are not the only helpers I have had on this day. As I stretched out the strings of lights on the front porch, my young husky pup decided it was he who was to be decorated. Wrapping himself in a cloak of many colours, he scurried about the yard, slightly out of my reach, proud of our newly invented game.

Now, I have made it sound like I do not enjoy this pre-holiday ritual. The truth is, none of the trials and tribulations of the exercise can take away from the end result — when the lights are up and you stand at the ready with audience gathered. You stick the plug into the socket. Your place lights up and the kids ooh and ahh, and bring to your attention the many lights that blink, flash, pop, and fade to black. It is back up to the roof.

Though one could argue that the intrinsic beauty of cottage country can be masked when the sun goes down, as it does quite early through December, the lights of Christmas tend to rectify this. Driving home in the evenings, along the back roads and lakeside drives, one marvels at the colourful strings of lights that trace out the rooflines of homes and cottages, frame windows and decks, wrap hedgerows and trees, and illuminate outdoor skating rinks. As a starry night in this region seems all the more brilliant because of the lack of big city lights, so, too, do the Christmas lights seem all the more acute. The lighting adds beauty and brilliance to cottage country. Twinkling stars and carefully laid out nativity scenes remind of us of Christmas's greatest story.

Traditions — they are a big part of the magic of the season, and bring back a powerful nostalgia for the family Christmas celebrations of our youth. I know we sometimes get cynical about the commercialism. At times we get overwhelmed by the shopping. We panic because the whole family is coming, and we want things to be perfect.

An escape to cottage country for Christmas is a great way to reconnect with holiday traditions and memories. Life at the cottage encourages fun in the snowy out-of-doors: sleigh rides and snowmobiles, skiing and tobogganing, and then sitting around a bonfire with a mug of hot chocolate. We clear skating rinks on the ponds and bays and enjoy an energetic shinny match. A snowman is built and stands guard. The distant sound of church bells and carolling is heard.

Inside, the cottage is warm and cozy, a fire burns in the hearth, and stockings are hung from the mantel. There is the scent of pine from a Christmas tree and fresh garland. A drink and some goodies are set out for Santa, and I assure the younger children that he will make it down the chimney just fine, in spite of the flames. There is the anticipation of Christmas morning, followed by the smell of the turkey, and a feast. There are mince pies, homemade fruitcake, and Christmas pudding. Best of all, there are family and friends.

Christmas in cottage country — it is Christmas-card perfect.

Gone Skiing

There were six pairs of cross-country skis under the Christmas tree this year. Six sets of backcountry skis, poles, and boots. Santa Claus must have felt I needed to get out and get a little more exercise. Well, not just me, my darling wife, too, and our four kids. Okay — he felt that I should, and he was kind enough to give me company.

I have not tried cross-country skiing for a good many years, not since my teenage years when the skis had just recently advanced past being wooden boards with leather straps. Way back then you had those vinyl/plastic low-cut boots that helped to deep freeze your toes into a painful state of numbness. You felt that if you whacked your foot with a ski pole, both boot and foot would crack in half. And that was on the warm winter days.

The equipment certainly has advanced. This new variety of boot is high-cut, leather, well-cushioned, and comfortably insulated. They look good too, racy and sleek. The long skis are a little wider than I remember, for ploughing down snowy trails. They are scaled on the bottom, so you no longer have to rub wax on them for hours before departure, pretending that you know what you are doing. Even the bindings seem much more sensible than the old "squeeze-the-toe" type that always seemed to pop loose as you were gaining speed down some steep pitch.

The gear advancements were well thought out. The equipment was, in my kids' words, "Sick!" That is good, by the way. All I needed now was a pair of spandex tights to complete the ensemble. Not. As my oldest girl would say, "Dad, just because I can pull the look off so well doesn't mean that you should even go there!"

I clip my boots into the ski bindings, grab the poles, and prepare to stride off down the peaceful trail. Instead, I lose my balance and fall clumsily into the soft, deep snow. I find out what the poles are actually for, as I slowly pry myself back to my feet and then fall the other way. My family waits patiently, if not quietly — I'm greeted by a chorus of heckling. I contemplate pulling out an excuse: a bad back, a sore knee, a concussion — I bonked my head and can't remember how my legs work. Instead I persevere, we are off, and I am soon mastering the technique.

My poles flick at the snow, working in unison with the skis. I push hard down the packed track; the dense groves of silver birch, maple, and aspen that hedge the trail are nothing more than a blur in my periphery. I

The sense of independence and self-sufficiency gained from skiing to the cottage in winter is deeply satisfying.

glide effortlessly along, climb up short hills, and then swoosh down long looping slopes that carve through thick stands of pine.

I begin wondering to myself whether there is enough time to prepare myself for the 2010 Vancouver Olympics. "Coming around the last corner, for Canada, well in the lead, is skier number thirteen in his flashy tight Lycra ski suit. Boy, does he look good. He is in great shape for a guy in his forties — it's hard to believe he just learned to ski last year, folks. What an effort — what an athlete …"

"Track!" I am brought back to the moment as my seven-year-old shouts, "Track!" and shuffles awkwardly past.

Okay, the Olympics are out. I am having fun, though, exploring cottage country like this, on skis with my family. The weather is pleasant. It is quiet, the heavy snow deadens any sound. Silence has even fallen over my loquacious wife and garrulous daughters as they concentrate on the effort. There is no sound save for my heavy breathing, the sound of wind, the twitter of the occasional bird.

The outing brought back fond memories from my youth, when I would ski along some tracked trail trying hard to stay in front of a prim and dainty girlfriend. Just as it became apparent that the race was lost and my manliness would be compromised, I would hail the girl over to the side of the trail for a slurp of a fine Chianti from a wineskin and some crusty, cold bread and cheese. Before departing for home I would push her over into the deep snow with the pretence of flirting, and then stride off down the winding path hoping to use the advantage of the head start to somehow stay in the lead. You see, everything for a man is a competition.

In those early days, my family made many treks to our island cottage in winter across the frozen, snow-covered lake, usually pulling our weekend's provisions behind us on toboggans. There were few things more satisfying than sitting back on the cottage porch with a hot toddy in hand, looking out over the pristine winter scene, knowing that you had earned this view, worked for the right to be here. The sense of independence and self-sufficiency gained from skiing to the cottage in winter was deeply satisfying. A few more outings like today and, the heck with the Olympics, my family and I will be ready for a cottage winter's journey.

In Stitches

I took a puck off the old nose the other day. I help coach a local team of young hockey players, and was probably throwing out some particularly invaluable piece of advice when a fellow coach's blistering snap shot rang off of the crossbar and then rang off of my tender schnozz. There I was, gushing red and scurrying off the ice at a speed that would have made Don Cherry proud.

It could have been worse. I could have taken it in the teeth or eye. It happened so quickly, but I did manage to turn enough that it hit me on the side of the nose rather than on the bone. So it wasn't broken, but split open badly enough that a good number of stitches were going to be required. With help, I bandaged the cut with hockey tape and gauze to slow the bleeding, then hopped in my truck for the hour and a half drive to the hospital.

For once, the accident didn't happen at the cottage, but it did happen at an arena in cottage country. For all of us who spend time at the cottage winter or summer, or who live in Muskoka year-round, there is always that little worry about medical facilities — will the doctor be in, or out on the golf course, canoeing down the river, fishing on the lake, out backcountry skiing on one of the beautiful trails, or off playing a game of shinny themselves? How long will we have to sit and wait, while our lifeblood slowly drains from our bodies?

I got in to see a doctor in a fairly timely manner. He seemed quite young to me, about half my age, but pleasant and personable. He took a look at my nose, let out a low whistle, and then immediately professed that he had to get a nose specialist, as this was beyond the scope of his expertise. He could stitch a finger or leg, maybe even a split noggin, but not a facial wound such as mine. Having made such a pronouncement, he left the little hospital room in search of a qualified nose-netician.

An hour later he was back. "Well," he said, "I guess I'll just have to do it." The closest nose, ear, and throat specialist he could find was in Barrie, but the stitches had to be done now, there was no time for the drive. "I'll give it a try," he said, to my mounting horror. "The helpful fellow in Barrie kind of told me how to do it."

And, just when I thought things could not get worse, in walked my darling wife, who saw me in my sorry state and started to laugh. The doctor got on his gloves and readied the needle and thread. My wife looked at my nose briefly and said, "Gross! I gotta go. I can't watch this." Before she walked out she turned to the doctor and threatened him, "Make sure you do a good job!" With that, out she stomped, and I saw the poor medical man start to shake. Sweat beads formed on his forehead.

So, with the doc trembling and me full of trepidation, he began his work, poking and threading together a split nostril on a nose barely frozen. I balled my fists and tried not to cry like a baby. He finished the first suture and then exclaimed, "Eeeeee, your wife's not going to like that, let me try that one again."

"Never mind my wife," I felt like shouting, "just get it done." But out it came, and then on he worked, jabbing, pulling, poking, and tying. Five stitches later he sat back and surveyed his work, satisfied with the outcome.

The doctor actually did a wonderful job. The nose is on straight and the cut is barely noticeable. And now the young professional has the experience and confidence to tackle the next facial laceration that walks in, someone who has fallen forward onto cross-country skis, tripped over a sleeping dog on the dock, or stumbled onto a jagged piece of rock while snowshoeing or hiking through our rugged cottage landscape.

For me it is just another little scar, a distinguishing mark, giving me a rugged look — or so I tell my wife. And the fine work the surgeon did is just another example of the quality of care we can expect to receive for any of those cuts and broken bones received during our time at the cottage, away from a major centre.

The End of Claus?

There is a certain magic in Christmas, mostly born of tradition. Though I'm sure every family approaches the holiday a little differently, for most, it is about family and home, friends and entertaining and giving. There are church bells and carolling, strings of lights around the home and stockings hung on the mantel, the scent of pine from a Christmas tree and fresh garland. There is the anticipation of Christmas morning, followed by the smell of the turkey, and a feast. There are mince pies, homemade fruitcake, and Christmas pudding. Every family has its own customs, but those little traditions become the memories and the touchstones that make Christmas so wonderful.

In the midst of all the holiday merriment last year, my youngest child, Jenna, then six years old, caught me completely off guard when she asked, "Dad, is there really a Santa Claus? So-and-so at school said he isn't real." I looked at her: her big green eyes told me that she wanted to know the truth, but she also was very hopeful that the truth was what she wanted.

This was not in line with those other queries: "Will Santa find us if we spend Christmas at the cottage?" Or "How will Santa make it down the chimney when you have the fire roaring?" No, this was a point-blank question about the truth. "Does Santa Claus really exist, or is it you and Mom that put all those presents under the tree and fill the stockings?" In other words, "Have you been lying to me all my life?"

It's that question that many parents fear, and coming from her, the youngest, it means the end of the line, the end of an era, the death of the jolly old man himself. Sure, you can tell her that the spirit of Santa Claus lives on, that he will always be a part of Christmas. No longer will there be that wide-eyed wonder, that child's absolute faith that Santa would arrive in the night, eat up the treats left for him, and crowd the bottom of the Christmas tree with presents for all the good boys and girls of the house.

Our oldest is fifteen now, so we have spent that many years perpetuating the myth. We would take it further. In the dark of night on Christmas Eve, I would sneak up on the roof and clop around like a team of reindeer. My wife's father would show up in a Santa Claus suit, ringing a bell and singing out, "Ho, ho, ho, Merry Christmas!"

We would let him in and he would chat with the girls, sounding a bit more like an old Chief of the Shuswap Nation addressing the Tribal Council than a jolly old elf from the North Pole. Our first child would screech mightily, and why not? Here was this funny looking, white-haired, bearded man dressed in a stylish red suit and sporting dark sunglasses to mask his true identity, showing up at the back door coaxing the youngster to come and sit on his lap with the promise of a present. We should have been proud of her trepidation, rather than insisting that she play along.

Fifteen years we have been able to enjoy the children and the Santa Claus story. Now here, with one simple question, it all would end. "Santa is half real, and half made up. He is real in here," I say, tapping her noggin. "He is part of your imagination. And because he is real in there, he is a very important part of all that is Christmas. Not the most important part, but an important part for both children and old guys like me." I expected anger (she is a bit strong-minded), or for her to be upset, but she simply smiled, nodded, and sauntered off.

Thankfully, we usually have lots of family around for Christmas. Jenna has her two young cousins visiting — later that same evening I hear her explaining to them that they must get to bed so Santa Claus will come. She tells them that she thought she saw Rudolph's red nose blinking in the night sky, leading the way into cottage country through a December snowfall. She helps them set out a little tray of snacks and a glass of milk.

Perhaps it never ends. When my oldest daughter reached that age where she realized we were fibbing about Santa, she just bought into the game. She kept the dream alive for her younger siblings. Ditto for the other children, who each in turn kept alive the magic. Someday they will spin it for their own children. Maybe, after all, Santa does indeed exist. He is a very real part of our Christmas psyches. Just listen very carefully, and you might hear the beat of reindeer hooves on the roof and the jolly laughter that warms a Christmas Eve night.

Winter Journey

It is during these short, cold, snowy January days that one starts to pine for summer at the cottage. I daydream about swimming in the lake, skiing, boating, drinking morning coffee on the dock, sitting in the Muskoka chair with a good book in the afternoon sun, and enjoying a bonfire in the evening — no longer dressed in boots and parka, just shorts, T-shirts, shades, and flip-flops.

Outside now, it is snowing and blowing, and I must bundle up, get out, and do a little more shovelling. There is, however, a certain beauty in this frozen world. I remember our first trek to the family cottage in winter. It was more than thirty-three years ago, shortly after my folks had purchased our island retreat. Crazy or brave, or perhaps simply adventurous, they had decided to take their four children on a long trek to visit the cabin in winter.

At that time, the backcountry roads were not kept open through the snowy months. We could drive our vehicle to within eighteen kilometres, no closer. We had no snowmobile. Our plan was to ski down the packed road and across the frozen lake, hauling our gear and provisions behind on toboggans, like Arctic adventurers on a trek to the Pole.

We set off in state of excitement, gliding down the trail, hauling our loads gamely up and down the sweeping hills. Pines were shrouded in heavy snow that blew off and swirled in the wind. Before we had travelled too far, our kid brother, tired from his hundred-metre walk, hitched a ride. The family basset hound trotted gamely ahead, but was not any help. Sometimes he would chase rabbits, falling off the packed trail, and we had to help him out of the deep powder.

We skied along for half the distance, and then removed the skis and tied them onto the sleds. Off came the ski boots, and we rubbed our frozen toes. We trudged on in winter boots. The miles stretched on, our exuberance waned, and our legs grew heavy. The first sight of the lake was like the first glimpse of water at the end of a long portage. With renewed energy we hopped on the loaded toboggans to glide down that long descent to the shore.

The lake in winter seemed even more remote and solitary, surrounded by stark, barren, trackless hills. It was also most serene on this late winter's afternoon when its snow-covered ice was deeply tinted with the gold of the setting sun. We had made it, but before we could get into the cottage we had to grab shovels and dig out the deep snow that had drifted in front of the door. We got a fire started in the box stove, not realizing that it would take hours to chase out the winter chill. Finally, exhausted, we huddled where the heat gathered first, high in the open loft, cuddling mugs of hot chocolate our mom had made.

Dad stoked the fire with maple and birch logs, and cooked up beef stew in the cast iron bean pot set on the fire. Toques, woollen mittens, snow pants, felt boot-liners, and parkas were hung from the loft railing to dry — the cottage looked like a laundry. The hound curled on the hearth rug, thawing and licking snow from between his pads. Gradually, the log walls soaked up the heat and gave the cottage a cozy warmth.

The next morning we shovelled a path to the privy and chopped a hole in the ice for water. We strapped on our beavertail snowshoes and headed out into the dense groves of naked birch and poplar, the snow-laden stands of pine, cedar, and balsam, that seemed so thick, black, and impenetrable. We dug snow forts, threw snowballs, and did some ice fishing.

Since I purchased the cottage, I have not made that winter trek with my own family. Hockey schedules, school activities, and weather seem to get in the way of dreamy plans. Perhaps this March we will put the skis on and set off on our own adventure. They plough the road right past the lake now, so it would only be a couple of kilometres across the frozen ice to the cabin. I have replaced the basset with huskies, and their passion

The passion of the huskies for their winter work transforms a trip to the cottage during the snowy months into a great adventure.

for winter work will make the journey easier — they will pull the gear. Perhaps it will be too easy and less memorable.

So, as I look outside my office window at the blustery Muskoka winter's day, I embrace the memories of that first winter journey to the cottage. It was a hard trek, but an unforgettable adventure.

The Cottage Rink

Every winter I debate with myself whether it is worthwhile to put all the time and effort into the building of a little backyard rink that the kids can enjoy. Every year I come to the conclusion that the rink is more effort than it is worth, more work than reward. There is a lot of shovelling, clearing, flooding, and building, and then when the rink is getting near perfect, the weather changes and warms and we get a little rain.

Still, when the cold weather comes in late November, I instinctively go out to put up the rink boards and set up the light standards that will allow the sheet of ice to get used after dark. Hockey dads are constantly trying to build the perfect backyard rink; boards and lighting and benches to tie skates, painted blue lines and red lines and regulation nets. One home rink nearby has PVC piping running from the home's eavestroughs to channel the fall rains onto the tarp catchment that covers the floor of the enclosed rink. It is a masterful way of flooding the ice.

We enjoyed a New Year's party last winter outside at another neighbourhood rink. It was big — not quite Olympic size, but certainly spacious. Boards surrounded the playing surface and fine netting was hung at either end as puck catchers. A large, long-handled squeegee was used to clean the snow off the ice between periods. Light standards allowed for after-dark play, and a roaring bonfire warmed the spectators, as did the hot rum toddies and the ring-in-the-new-year champagne.

Then there are the attempts at manufacturing the perfect ice flooding machine. While I use the old garden hose method, water dribbling out and freezing solid to my gloves, others have built fancy, portable, hand-operated rink waterers, steel pipe frames with attached rubber mats that distribute the water evenly. Some have taken this a step further and tried to attach these systems to their lawn tractors.

While the dads have aspirations as Zamboni drivers, the youngsters would rather aspire to be their hockey heroes. This one shows up in a Crosby jersey, that one has a Stamkos Lightning sweater, and these two siblings have Doughty and Weber Team Canada wear. This finely appointed bright young fellow wears Leafs colours, while that slightly misguided dunce wears the *bleu et rouge* of the much-hated Habs, so I don't allow him to play … just kidding.

The outdoor rink cleared on the cottage lake is the ultimate in Canadiana. All you need here is a well-frozen bay or pond, and some help from Mother Nature. She needs to serve up some bitterly cold weather before sending us her snow. Often the cottage rink is a shared venture, with many neighbours helping to clear and maintain the ice, sometimes drilling holes and then flooding the rink with portable pumps. And the more the merrier when an energetic shinny match is played.

A couple years back we took our small-town Atom-aged hockey team on an overnight getaway to a bayside cottage off the French River. It was a perfect year weather-wise for ice. The temperatures had turned biting cold for a whole week until the bay had frozen solid and smooth as glass. Any snow that fell afterwards was swept away by the wind, blown into drifts along the shore. The skating rink was perfect. We set up two nets and divided up the players and then we played … no offsides, no rules, we didn't keep score.

At first we had boundaries fixed in our heads, about half the size of a small arena, net to net with some space behind. As we got heated, jackets were discarded and left as markers where the sideboards might have been. Then a puck was fired hard and wide and it glided off over the ice. Suddenly the game spilled over into the endless space, players with sticks and toques skated in a jumble over the frozen lake.

While the adults took a break, the kids skated off for miles in a straight line and shot pucks that no arena boards would confine. They skated fast and hard and jumped skiffs of blown snow, tripping and hooking each other, laughing and playing the ultimate game of keep-away. No referees, no coaches, no rules, and no parents yelling from the stands, nobody taking it too seriously. Just freedom and speed and movement and grace, outside in the cool, crisp air. The cold and the winter wind put a glow on their cheeks.

And when they had skated their miles, had covered every corner of the frozen bay, they skated back to the warmth of the bonfire for hot chocolate and to catch their breaths. Once warmed, they were off again, darting like the summer water-bugs, this way and that over the ice. It was beautiful. It was the best of hockey, a game of shinny on the cottage rink.

Cottage Dreaming

Men never grow up. They think and act like children. That is my conclusion, having conducted recent research.

The Spring Cottage Life Show at the tail end of winter is the stage for my investigations. It is the perfect time to check out all the new cottage products, the toys and gadgets that, in our minds, will add both comfort and excitement to our summer days. I'm especially excited this year because we have brought the kids along — which means more fun for a dad than simply having to trail after a spouse on an agonizing stop-and-go trek through the endless aisles of Martha Stewart–like interior exhibits. No, cottage life should be about fun in the outdoors, not inside entertaining. The kids won't put up with the monotony of furniture, crafts, and cutesy knick-knacks, I reason. Meaning this visit will be about fun and toys and ... then comes the letdown, in one simple sentence.

"Why don't you kids wander around on your own, and we can meet back here in an hour? Your dad and I want to check out the new cottage kitchens."

No! They will be climbing in and out of fancy new boats, checking out the latest in canoes, kayaks, catamarans, and windsurfers, sitting dreamily on Jet Skis and hiking themselves out on some racy sailboat like a crew-hand in the America's Cup. They will lounge briefly in the cushioned seats of pontoon boats and play with the steering wheel of a ritzy cabin cruiser while envisioning themselves as some multi-millionaire yacht owner. They will be kicked off a good many vessels by salesmen wanting to impress more legitimate customers. The kids will try on the latest water skis and boogie boards, bounce on water trampolines, practise fly casting, and try to climb into futuristic hot tubs. I want to be with them.

Challenging a lake that is as still as glass.

Instead, my wife and I are hanging out staring at soapstone countertops that are "as attractive as they are durable and not only impervious to heat and stains, but virtually maintenance free." I run over to a wine tasting exhibit to help me get through this, and then catch up to my darling wife drooling over a mammoth pine harvest table with eight sturdy plank chairs. "Wouldn't this look good at the cabin?" she seems to be asking me, and I would probably hear her, were I not looking off with envy in the direction my four youngsters wandered.

She stops and listens to some talking head extolling the virtues of something called ShamWow!, and then I see her take out her wallet. She hands me a small, square piece of very expensive felt and tells me she bought it for me to clean our old boat — "Fellow said it would be just like new!" I run back over to the wine exhibit, swirl a Shiraz around in my mouth, and tell the person who poured it, "Ah, full-bodied, with a distinct note of black cherry and a hint of pepper, if I'm not mistaken," or some such thing that I memorized from the information card.

We meander through some food exhibits and sample feta-stuffed mini pitas and little nibbles of chocolate cashew buttercrunch, so small that they are only a tease. We dip pretzels into little dishes of various sauces, while a lady explains to my wife the fine ingredients whilst glaring at me, undoubtedly recognizing the classic vacant look of the typical double-dipper. A spicy chili concoction has me running back to the vintner exhibit, only to find that I have been cut off.

Finally, mercifully, the hour is up, and we hasten back to the rendezvous point. Perhaps seeing my pain and sensing my agony, my compassionate children beg me to come with them for a brief look at all they have discovered. I cast my eye on the elegant lines and shining chrome of a polished mahogany launch. The kids drag me onward to the fancy ski boat with all the bells and whistles, especially the enormous stereo speakers that I'm sure would be heard all around the lake. If that's not loud enough for them, they marvel at a jet boat. With exclamations of approval, my son watches a video clip that shows the enormous, space-age craft zooming around a lake, belching fire out of its back end and sending a plume of spray a hundred metres in its wake.

My wife stares dreamily at a sporty Hobie Cat, I'm sure taking her back to the sailing days of her youth. There is a sleek wooden rowboat, and I imagine rowing it around the island and over to shore each morning, a great way to get into shape. I show it to my wife, who imagines herself sprawled out in the bow sipping red wine while I get into shape. Something new for the cottage dream list, somewhere ahead of the flatulent jet boat, but surely well behind a harvest table.

Epilogue: My Happy Place

It is a hot afternoon at the lake, very warm and quite humid. The air is still and hazy, and the lake is like glass. Only occasionally does a breath of wind ripple the water and cause the pine branches overhead to nod gently. This breeze offers a brief respite from the heat, and from the little flies that tickle your legs and nip at your ankles.

I have tucked myself back into the shade of the tree to watch the kids at play in the lake and to leaf through a good book. My daughters paddle their kayaks around our small bay like synchronized dancers, weaving in and out and around one another. Sometimes they splash one another with their paddles, all the while giggling and having fun.

When I feel a little too hot, I'll wander down to the dock and slip off the end. The water envelops me. It is cool and refreshing. I swim out twenty strokes and then return. Before reaching the dock I dive under the water and head for the kayaks, hoping to attack them from beneath and dump their contents into the lake. They see me coming, however, and dart off laughing. I climb out, towel myself off, and return to the shade.

The dogs are curled beneath the boughs of a full spruce, hiding from the heat and the biting flies. They don't even lift their heads as I pass, but acknowledge me with a couple of thumps of their tails. They have run all morning and now rest exhausted and content.

I saunter up to the fridge in the cabin and grab a cold beer for myself and a cider for my wife. We sit on the dock together, watching our four children frolicking in the clear lake water, and we actually talk. We talk about things other than work. We don't mention the kids' long list of activities, or try to work out the complicated logistics of their daily schedules at home, of getting each child to where they need to be: piano, dance, soccer, hockey, baseball, track and field, dental and doctor appointments, tutors, or movie theatres. Rather, we talk about dreams and ideas, projects and schemes.

We talk about the future and reminisce about the past. Some memories make us both laugh. I look at my wife's radiant smile and her twinkling brown eyes and remember why I fell for her those many years ago.

My son and I cook up some ribs on the barbecue for dinner, together. While I sip on a mug of Irish pale ale, he stands beside me with a tin of root beer. We have our baseball caps pulled down low and sunglasses shading our eyes. He slathers some sauce over the ribs with a basting brush and then turns them with the tongs. The dogs offer to help out, but we order them away.

After dinner we all help clean up the kitchen, and then we pull out the old Clue game. It is fun playing now that the kids are our equals. It is nice that they are at that age when we can try our hardest, yet they still manage to outwit us.

They also seem able to outlast us in the night, possibly because they don't often rise until near noon. We bid them good night, give them their flashlights and books, and they disappear down to the boathouse bunkie. I blow out the kerosene lamps in the cabin and crawl under the feather comforter and snuggle up to my wife in our log bed.

I file the day in the image bank of my mind. When I'm away and overrun at work I can recall it. When it is the dead of winter, which can be ferocious, cold, and long in these parts, I can sit back in my office chair, think about this day, and smile. When the people around me are simply being unreasonable, I can pull the image out of my mind's file and it will cheer me.

*Fun enough to
last the full year.*

My wife might find me looking vacant and grinning inanely, but rather than call me a dreamy-looking idiot she will kindly ask, "Have you gone off to your happy place?"

Of Related Interest

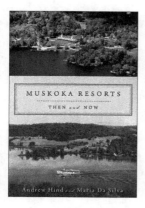

Muskoka Resorts
Then and Now
by Andrew Hind and Maria Da Silva
978-1554888573
$25.00

Nature's Year
*Changing Seasons in Central and
Eastern Ontario*
by Drew Monkman
978-1459701830
$34.99

Since the 1880s, people have travelled to Muskoka in search of solace and relaxation, enjoying the comfortable confines and warm welcome of resorts while at the same time revelling in the tranquil wilderness and refreshing lakes. Things haven't really changed all that much over the past century. This storied past of carefree summers and timeless hospitality is the focus of *Muskoka Resorts*. Twenty classic resorts are explored, some of which are thriving today, such as Windermere House and Deerhurst, while others such as Limberlost and Bigwin Inn are long gone, though fondly remembered.

This almanac of key events in nature occurring in Central and Eastern Ontario covers a region that extends from the Bruce Peninsula and Georgian Bay in the west to Ottawa and Cornwall in the east. The book is a chronicle of the passing seasons designed to inform cottagers, gardeners, photographers, suburban backyard birders, and nature enthusiasts alike as to what events in nature to expect each month of the year.